NAOMI LANE

MEDITERRANEAN
AIR FRYER

Healthy Recipes to fry, grill, bake and Roast
Even for **One** & **Two**

**200
EFFORTLESS
RECIPES**

Photo by Emiliano Vittoriosi

Table of Content

Introduction

INTRODUCTION

This cookbook deals with everything you need to know about the Mediterranean diet, taking full advantage of the amazing air fryer, which enables you to prepare some easy, mouthwatering, and both tender and crispy dishes.

Imagine that you are in a beautiful restaurant on the sunny shores of the Mediterranean, the sea joining the sky, the sun reflecting on the sea, and sea sodium's scent. In front of you is a healthy meal consisting of fish, fresh vegetables, and excellent olive oil, natural food that comes directly from local producers, with no processed food—just you and nature.

If you can imagine it, this is why the Mediterranean Diet is ranked as the healthiest diet in the world. Olive oil, fish, vegetables, seeds, fruit, sun and earth, and a beautiful smile.

The proof is the people who live on the Mediterranean coasts called "Blue Zones." They manage to live past 100 in health and without problems.

The Mediterranean is a source of health and well-being. I wanted to take some of the freshest Mediterranean recipes and re-adapt them to the Air fryer in this book.

Starting a diet is not always easy for some; organizing meals and studying can often be frustrating.

After countless consultations with my patients, I have realized that one of the main problems is the difficulty of preparing meals.

Imagine taking the ingredients and placing them in your Air fryer, setting the temperature, and letting it do all the work. No stress. The only thing you have to do is enjoy the meal.

The Air fryer will be your best ally.

The recipes are designed to be prepared at home with easy-to-find ingredients. Quickly prepare for those who don't have time and those who don't have much cooking knowledge. All recipes have been tested directly by me.

This book is for those who want to do the Mediterranean Diet to lose weight and get in shape, but also for those who simply want to take a trip to the Mediterranean and discover tastes and flavors rich in history, sun, and sea.

I hope the recipes introduced in this cookbook will be enjoyed by all and help you to maintain a healthy lifestyle.

The Mediterranean diet is not a market gambit or some predefined rule that you need to follow; rather **it is a pure lifestyle.**

The Mediterranean Diet and Air Fryer Essentials

The Mediterranean diet is all about simple, whole, and natural food items, based around organic produce with no artificial and processed items. The word Mediterranean makes us think about sunny beaches, fresh air, and nature. The food included in the diet is not only healthy but also delicious as it is close to nature, and the human body is developed to eat natural food. The diet is adopted from the people living near the coast of the Mediterranean Sea, including France, Spain, Turkey, Italy, Greece, Morocco, and Israel.

The basic aim of the Mediterranean diet is to eat fresh seasonal fruits, seasonal vegetables, nuts, oil, seeds, whole grains, seafood, and red wine. This diet fully supports and appreciates the eating habits of the Mediterranean people.

One important thing to note is that the consumption of pork is not recommended. The Mediterranean diet also encourages regular exercise or some daily physical activity.

Now, let us look at the history of the Mediterranean diet.

History of the Mediterranean Diet

The Mediterranean diet is all about seasonal food items that are found in the Mediterranean countries.

It was 1945 when Dr Ancel Keys, an American physiologist, started to study the Mediterranean diet. He introduced a seven-country study in 1958, which focused on the relationship between a healthy heart and a healthy lifestyle. His research and analysis revealed that the death rates in America and its regional countries were far higher than in European countries. He further stressed that differences between the lifestyle and eating habits of both continents was the key factor. After his study, the diet of the Mediterranean caught the eye of many others, and people start appreciating and recognizing the benefits of the lifestyle and eating habits.

Pyramid of the Mediterranean Diet

The pyramid of the Mediterranean diet is based on the eating choices of people living in the Mediterranean. Listed below are food pyramid guidelines that are developed to encourage people to follow this diet.
The Mediterranean diet pyramid reduces the risk of diabetes, stroke, and other underlying illnesses.
You should base every meal around

- Vegetables and fruits
- Legumes
- Grains
- Beans

- Nuts
- Seeds
- Olive oil
- Eat fish twice a week
- Eat a moderate amount of poultry, fish, dairy, cheese, eggs
- Red wine: 1 glass per day for women, and 2 glasses per day for men

Eat less:
- Red meat
- Saturated fat
- Sweets

Benefits of a Mediterranean Diet

The Mediterranean diet is full of benefits; some of them are listed below.

- The Mediterranean diet leads to a healthier heart.
- The Mediterranean diet helps to achieve a healthy blood sugar level and counteracts diabetes.
- The Mediterranean diet supports physical activities that help reduce weight.
- While following Mediterranean diet you feel less stress and anxiety.
- The diet helps in maintaining a healthy gut.
- It helps to control hypertension and reduce the risk of heart diseases.
- The Mediterranean diet helps lower bad cholesterol.
- Because of the healthy food pyramid, the diet tends to have a remarkable effect on the brain and heart health.

- The Mediterranean diet makes you feel full and satisfied.
- This diet helps you stop binge eating.
- The Mediterranean diet is rich in fruits and vegetables, so it helps in reducing inflammation and related diseases.

Tips for Creating a Mediterranean Diet Plan

Listed below are some useful tips that will help anyone to successfully start a Mediterranean diet plan.

- Consider vegetables and fruits the staple of your diet. They help detoxify the body and make you much healthier.
- Fruit juices should be limited to 120ml a day because of their high sugar content.
- Vegetable salad should be added to the meal plan.
- Replace all white flour with wholegrain flour.
- Use minimal or no processed and refined grains. All organic and whole-grains are allowed, such as wheat, rice, couscous, barley, polenta, millet, faro, and oats.
- Include low-fat dairy items in the diet.
- Focus should be on low-fat milk, Greek yogurt, and some amount of cheese.
- Eat fish daily.
- Drink 5-227g of red wine if you want to.
- Go for healthy fat options like olive oil, and avocado oil.
- Eat a handful of nuts when you feel like a snack.
- Leave out the pork and limit intake of red meat.

- Add more whole-grains and legumes to your meal.
- Limit salt intake.
- Don't be a couch potato: bring more movement into your life.
- Avoid eating processed food, artificially flavored, and canned food.
- It is important to balance the food ratio of omega 3, and omega 6.

Healthy Snack Options for a Mediterranean Diet

- Nuts (handful)
- Seeds
- Fruits (organic and fresh)
- Vegetables like carrots/cucumber
- Greek yogurt
- Peanut/almond butter
- Organic Berries

Air Fryer Essential

This section deals with the air fryer and its use, to help beginners to understand the appliance. The air fryer can prepare crispy, delicious, homemade food with a hands-free cooking experience.

If you are a busy person who loves cooking but lacks the time to prepare food, then this appliance will be perfect for you. It is one of the easiest appliances to work with, and will cook you a low-calorie meal with just a teaspoon of oil added to the food. It does not drain out the nutrients, or saturate food with fat like deep fryers.

For a better understanding of how it works let's start with the basics of an air fryer.

What is an Air Fryer, and How Does it Work?

An air fryer is one of the top trending appliances for the modern kitchen. It cooks food by circulating hot air around the food. The air fryer requires very little oil to make food crispy on the outside and moist on the inside. The heat is usually circulated up to 200°C (390°F) around a very thin layer of oil coating the food, resulting in crispy and moist food that is ready to serve.

Air Fryer FAQs

Q. Is cooking in an air fryer healthy?
A. Of course, an air fryer is one of the healthiest appliances around; it cooks food in 80% less oil, making it one of the best choices for the health conscious.

Q. Do I have to put a lot of oil in an air fryer?
A. Not at all, as the basic purpose of the air fryer is to use very little oil but get the same results as deep fryers.

Q. Can you put any sort of paper inside the air fryer?
A. Yes, it is safe to use parchment paper, butter paper, or even aluminium foil while cooking food.

Q. Do air fryers cause cancer?
A. No, it is a very safe appliance, and it doesn't affect the body in a bad way. The risk of cancer is reduced as the level of acrylamide is 90% less in items that are air-fried rather than deep-fried.

Q. Is the air fryer dishwasher safe?

A. The removable parts of the air fryer are dishwasher safe. It is not, of course, recommended to submerge the whole appliance in water, as it is an electrical appliance.

How to Clean the Air Fryer

The cleaning of the air fryer is very easy as most of the parts of the air fryer are dishwasher safe.

- It is highly recommended to clean the basket of the air fryer after every use.
- When you clean the air fryer, let the appliance cool off completely first, and then take out all its removable parts.
- Use a damp cloth to wipe the exterior of the fryer.
- Use a dishwasher to wash the removable parts, or you can use a dishwashing liquid and sponge to wash them manually and then rinse under the tap.
- If food particles are stuck to the air fryer, use a soft scrub or brush to scrape out the residual bits.
- Use lukewarm water for cleaning, as it is more effective.

Tips on How to Cook Well with an Air Fryer

- Wash the air fryer before using it for the first time.
- Adjust the air fryer so that it is level, on a flat surface in the kitchen.
- Leave some space behind the appliance, so the heat created has room to escape.

- Breading and coating the food with oil spray is crucial, as hot air is circulated around the food.
- The correct accessories should be used when making cakes, pastries, or casseroles in the air fryer. The accessory pans should be fitted inside the air fryer.
- Use drawers inside the air fryer when cooking fatty food, to prevent grease converting into smoke.
- Remember to flip the food halfway through cooking.
- Make sure the air fryer is completely dry after cleaning and washing.
- It is not recommended to overcrowd the appliance basket with food.

What <u>Not</u> to Put in the Air Fryer

- Simple cheese
- Raw beans and grains
- Wet battered food items

Different Types of Air Fryers

Which air fryer you decide to purchase merely depends on your own needs and budget. The size and additional features are the most important things to keep in mind. Here are some examples of what you might get for your money (at time of writing):

- Cuisinart Air fryer, Convection Toaster Air fryer, Silver, Dial Buttons, 16 litres. Price: £470.
- COSORI Air Fryer Max XL, LED, 5.5 litres, Price £107.99.
- Philips Air fryer, Avance Turbo Star, Digital, Black, HD9641/96, Buttons/LED, 0.82 litres. Price £107.

- Ninja Foodi 7-in-1 Multi-Cooker, 6 litres, OP300UK. Price: £199.99.
- Lakeland Digital Compact Air Fryer, compact size, ideal for two people. Price £74.99
- Tower Digital Air Fryer 4.3 litres. Price £75.

Useful Accessories for Mediterranean Recipes

- Skillets and cooking pans
- Parchment liners/butter papers
- Racks
- Small grill plates
- Full air fryer accessories pack

Oatmeal Flax Muffins

Prep: 15 Minutes | Cook Time: 15 Minutes | Makes: 2 Servings

Dry Ingredients:
1 cup wheat flour
1 cup oats
½ cup sugar
2 tablespoons flax seed powder
1 teaspoon cinnamon
1 teaspoon baking powder
½ teaspoon baking soda
¼ teaspoon salt

Wet Ingredients:
½ cup almond milk
1 egg
3 tablespoons extra virgin olive oil
¼ teaspoon vanilla extract
1 ripened banana, peeled

Preheat the air fryer to 400°F. Put muffin liners in the muffin cups.
In a mixing bowl, add the dry ingredients and mix them well.
Take a separate bowl and whisk all the wet ingredients, then mix together with dry ingredients.
Pour the mixture into the muffin cups.
Bake the muffins for 15 minutes.
Serve, and enjoy as a delicious breakfast.

Calories 920 Total Fat 32.4g Saturated Fat 5.1g Cholesterol 87mg Sodium 677mg Total Carbohydrate 147.2g Dietary Fiber 11g Total Sugars 60.8g Protein 19.3g

Turkey Filled Omelets

Prep: 10 Minutes | Cook Time: 6 Minutes | Makes: 2 Servings

1 tablespoon olive oil
1 tablespoon shiitake mushroom
1 chopped shallot
¼ teaspoon salt
1 sage leaf
1/2 teaspoon crushed red pepper flakes
1/2 cup shredded cooked turkey
2 eggs
1/8 teaspoon white pepper
2 teaspoons olive oil
1 tablespoon crème Fraiche

Take a skillet and add oil over medium heat. Add the chopped mushroom to the skillet along with sage, shallot, red pepper flakes, and salt. Cook the mushroom for 5 minutes. Then stir in the shredded turkey and cook for a few minutes. Put this to one side to cool. Meanwhile, whisk the eggs with salt and white pepper in a small bowl. Once completely cool, add the turkey ingredients to the eggs. Take a round cake pan, grease it with oil and pour the egg mixture into the pan. Add cake pan to air fryer basket and cook for 6 minutes at 204°C (400°F). Once cooked, remove it from the pan and place the crème fraîihe on top.

Calories 193 Total Fat 13.4g Saturated Fat 3g Cholesterol 190 mg Sodium 378 mg Total Carbohydrate 2.4g Dietary Fibre 0.6g Total Sugars 0.6g Protein 16.4g

Air Fryer Egg Cups

Prep: 5 Minutes | Cook Time: 10 Minutes | Makes: 4 Servings

5 eggs
½ cup cream
½ cup of cheddar
1/2 pound sausage
1 teaspoon olive oil
1 teaspoon garlic cloves
2 cups spinach

Take a skillet and add ground sausage. Cook for 15 minutes over medium heat. Once cooked, keep the crumbled sausage aside. Now, add oil to the skillet and sauté garlic until fragrant. Then add the spinach to the skillet and cook until it wilts; leave on one side to cool down. Meanwhile, beat the eggs with the milk, and add cheese, spinach, and cooked sausage. Place the egg mixture into oiled muffin cups and cook at 350°F, for 10 minutes. Once it is ready, serve and enjoy!

Calories 329 Total Fat 25.4g Saturated Fat 8.7g Cholesterol 261mg Sodium 610 mg Total Carbohydrate 2.4g Dietary Fibre 0.3g Total Sugars 1.2g   Protein 22.1g

Mediterranean Frittata

Prep: 8 Minutes | Cook Time: 12 Minutes | Makes: 3 Servings

6 eggs
1/2 cup heavy cream
4-ounces Cheddar Cheese
1 bell pepper
1cup sliced mushrooms
5 slices cooked bacon
salt and pepper, to taste
Chives (optional)

Take a mixing bowl and beat the eggs with cream.
Now, add the cheese, bacon, bell pepper, and mushrooms.
Place the mixture in the greased baking pan, and put the pan in the air fryer basket.
Add seasonings such as salt and pepper and bake at 177°C (350°F) for 12 minutes.
Sprinkle the cooked frittata with chopped chives.

Calories 537 Total Fat 42.1g Saturated Fat 19.7g Cholesterol 429 mg Sodium 1100 mg Total Carbohydrate 6g Dietary Fibre 0.8g Total Sugars 3.3g Protein 33.8g

Air Fryer Breakfast feta Pizza

Prep: 10 Minutes | Cook Time: 5 Minutes | Makes: 2 Servings

1 whole-wheat pizza dough
4 scrambled eggs
Few Sausage
1/2 bell pepper, chopped
1 cup feta cheese

Grease the baking pan with oil.
Place the dough in the baking pan and keep it in the air fryer.
Cook for 5 minutes at 350°F.
Once cooked, top it with peppers, scrambled eggs, cooked sausage, and cheese.
Serve the pizza and enjoy!

Calories 476 Daily Total Fat 31.6g Saturated Fat 16.8g Cholesterol 410mg Sodium 1218mg Total Carbohydrate 19.3g Dietary Fibre 2.4g Total Sugars 7.8g Protein 27.4g

Prosciutto & Spinach Egg Cups

Prep: 10 Minutes | Cook Time: 10 Minutes | Makes: 2 Servings

5 prosciutto slices
Oil spray, for greasing
6 eggs
1/2 cup baby spinach
Black pepper and salt, to taste

Preheat the air fryer to 350°F. Place the prosciutto slices in the oiled muffin cups. Then place the spinach leaves on top, and pour the beaten eggs into the cup. Sprinkle with pepper and salt.
Keep it in the air fryer basket and bake the eggs for 10 minutes. Once ready, serve and enjoy!

Calories 501 Total Fat 25.2g Saturated Fat 8g Cholesterol 604mg Sodium 2747mg Total Carbohydrate 4.5g Dietary Fibre 0.2g Total Sugars 1.1g Protein 61.3g

Easy Greek Frittata (GF)

Prep: 15 Minutes | Cook Time: 12 Minutes | Makes: 2 Servings

Cooking spray
4 eggs
3 tablespoons whipping cream
1 cup spinach leaves
½ cup feta cheese
1 cup cherry tomatoes
½ cup diced onion
1 teaspoon dried oregano
salt and black pepper, to taste

Preheat an air fryer to 177°C (350°F) for a few minutes.
Grease the cake pan with cooking spray. Take a mixing bowl and beat the eggs with the cream. Then add spinach, onion, oregano, feta cheese, cherry tomatoes, salt, and pepper. Pour the mixture into the cake pan and cover it with aluminium foil from the top.
Cook the frittata for 12 minutes in the air fryer; serve and enjoy.

Calories 324 Total Fat 24g Saturated Fat 12.7g Cholesterol 386mg Sodium 567mg Total Carbohydrate 10.1g Dietary Fibre 2.4g Total Sugars 5.9g Protein 18.5g

Spinach and feta Egg Casserole (GF)

Prep: 10 Minutes | Cook Time: 22 Minutes | Makes: 2 Servings

1 tablespoon olive oil
1/2 yellow onion
1/2 diced red bell pepper
2 teaspoons kosher salt
6 ounces baby spinach
2 crushed garlic cloves
2 tablespoons dill
10 eggs
2 cups almond milk
1 tablespoon Dijon mustard
1/4 teaspoon black pepper
5 ounces feta cheese

Preheat the air fryer to 350°F. Grease the baking dish with oil.
Add oil to the skillet and sauté the pepper and onion, adding a little salt to it to help it caramelise. Then add the garlic and spinach and cook for a further 3 minutes. Once the spinach wilts, add the dill and transfer it to the baking dish. In a mixing bowl, beat the eggs with milk, pepper, salt, and mustard. Whisk it well.
Pour the mixture in the pan over spinach and sprinkle the feta cheese all over it. Bake the casserole for 22 minutes or until it gets brown. Serve and enjoy!

Calories 742 Total Fat 49.9g Saturated Fat 21.5g Cholesterol 901mg Sodium 3704mg Total Carbohydrate 27.8g Dietary Fibre 3.6g Total Sugars 18.7g Protein 49.8g

Spinach, feta, and Pepper Omelette (GF)

Prep: 10 Minutes | Cook Time: 12 Minutes | Makes: 2 Servings

1 tablespoon olive oil
4 eggs
2 tablespoons half and half
salt and pepper
1/2 teaspoon garlic powder
1/2 cup bell peppers chopped
1 cup spinach
1/2 cup feta cheese

Preheat the air fryer to 350°F.Take a mixing bowl and add the eggs, salt, pepper, and the milk and cream. Whisk together and keep to one side. In a skillet add bell peppers and olive oil over medium heat. Cook for 2 minutes then add some salt, black pepper, garlic powder, and the spinach. Cook for another 2 minutes, then transfer it to a plate and let it cool down. In the baking pan that fits inside the basket of the air fryer, pour in the egg mixture, and add all the cooled skillet ingredients. Cook it in the air fryer basket for 8 minutes at 204°C (400°F). Once it is completely cooked, spread the cheese over the omelette. Serve warm and enjoy!

Calories 501 Total Fat 25.2g Saturated Fat 8g Cholesterol 604mg Sodium 2747mg Total Carbohydrate 4.5g Dietary Fibre 0.2g Total Sugars 1.1g Protein 61.3g

Air Fryer Vegetable Omelette (GF)

Prep: 12 Minutes | Cook Time: 10 Minutes | Makes: 2 Servings

2 eggs
1/4 cup milk
salt, to taste
½ cup Veggies of your choice
1/2 cup shredded mozzarella cheese

Take a mixing bowl, add the eggs and milk, and whisk well. Add salt and chopped veggies to the egg mixture. Pour the mixture into the greased pan. Keep the pan in the air fryer and cook at 350°F for 10 minutes. When it is half cooked, add cheese to the Omelette. Serve warm and enjoy!

Calories 742 Total Fat 49.9g Saturated Fat 21.5g Cholesterol 901mg Sodium 3704mg Total Carbohydrate 27.8g Dietary Fibre 3.6g Total Sugars 18.7g Protein 49.8g

Air Fryer Egg Bites (GF)

Prep: 10 Minutes | Cook Time: 15 Minutes | Makes: 2 Servings

4 eggs
2 tablespoons coconut milk
2 tablespoons green onions, chopped
Salt and black pepper
1/4 cup shredded cheese

Grease the ramekin dish with cooking spray. Add the chopped onions and place the dish in the air fryer. Cook the onions at 340° for 5 minutes. Meanwhile, mix together eggs, milk, salt and pepper in a mixing bowl. Once the onion is cooked, pour the egg mixture in the dish and top it with cheese. Cook the whole thing for 8 minutes at 360°F. Serve and enjoy!

Calories 742 Total Fat 49.9g Saturated Fat 21.5g Cholesterol 901mg Sodium 3704mg Total Carbohydrate 27.8g Dietary Fibre 3.6g Total Sugars 18.7g Protein 49.8g

Vegan Sweet Potato Fritters

Prep: 15 Minutes | Cook Time: 12 Minutes | Makes: 4 Servings

2 cups shredded sweet potato/ yams
1 cup almond flour
½ cup diced onions
1 tablespoon olive oil
½ teaspoon salt
½ teaspoon black pepper
¼ teaspoon turmeric powder
Avocado oil cooking spray

Preheat the air fryer to 177°C 350°F. Take a mixing bowl and add onions, olive oil, salt, shredded sweet potato, almond flour, pepper, and turmeric. Mix well. Make patties out of the potato mixture.
Arrange the patties in the air fryer basket that is greased with oil spray. Cook for 12 minutes and flip the patties halfway through cooking. Once both sides are cooked, serve the patties with sauce and enjoy!

Calories 398 Total Fat 26.8g Saturated Fat 3.6g Cholesterol 0mg
Sodium 340mg Total Carbohydrate 32.6g Dietary Fibre 10.1g
Total Sugars 7.4g Protein 9.2g

Crispy Quinoa Cakes

Prep: 4h 10 Minutes | Cook Time: 8 Minutes | Makes: 4 Servings

3 cups cold cooked quinoa
1 cup grated carrot
1 cup grated Parmesan cheese
2 tablespoons basil
2 garlic cloves
½ teaspoon salt
½ teaspoon black pepper
3 medium eggs
¾ cup Panko
3 tablespoons olive oil

Take a mixing bowl and add eggs, quinoa, garlic, salt, carrot, Parmesan, basil, pepper, and eggs and mix it well. Then add breadcrumbs and make patties out of the mixture. Place the patties in the greased baking tray and refrigerate for 4 hours. Line the patties into an oiled air fryer basket. Cook it for 8 minutes, flipping halfway through. Garnish the patties with basil and serve. Enjoy!

Calories 724 Total Fat 24.1g Saturated Fat 4.7g Cholesterol 128mg
Sodium 576mg Total Carbohydrate 100.3g Dietary Fibre 10.6g
Total Sugars 2.9g Protein 27.5g

Cinnamon-Cake Doughnut Holes

Prep: 12 Minutes | Cook Time: 8 Minutes | Makes: 4 Servings

2 cups whole wheat flour
¼ cup sugar
1 teaspoon baking powder
¼ teaspoon salt
4 tablespoons butter
¼ cup milk
2 teaspoons cinnamon

Take a mixing bowl and add flour, sugar, salt, and baking powder. Then add milk and butter, and mix thoroughly to form a dough. Knead it well. Then make small balls out of the dough mixture.
Line the air fryer basket with parchment paper. Now, roll the balls in the cinnamon and sugar mixture. Bake the balls at 350°F for 8 minutes. Serve warm balls and enjoy!

Calories 388 Total Fat 12.5g Saturated Fat 7.6g Cholesterol 32mg
Sodium 239mg Total Carbohydrate 62.5g Dietary Fibre 2.3g
Total Sugars 13.4g Protein 7.1g

Air Fryer Chocolate Croissants

Prep: 10 Minutes | Cook Time: 10 Minutes | Makes: 2 Servings

1 package whole wheat crescent rolls, organic and vegan
4 tablespoons of dark chocolate
2 tablespoons coconut oil
Powdered sugar

Directions melt chocolate with coconut oil in a small pan. Preheat the air fryer to 350°F for 5 minutes. Cut the roll into triangles and add the chocolate mixture to the roll. Roll up and seal the edges.
Place the croissants in the preheated air fryer and bake for approximately 6 mins. Once croissants are baked enough, dust with icing sugar. Serve and enjoy!

Calories 398 Total Fat 26.8g Saturated Fat 3.6g Cholesterol 0mg
Sodium 340mg Total Carbohydrate 32.6g Dietary Fibre 10.1g
Total Sugars 7.4g Protein 9.2g

Cheese Stuffed Crescent Rolls

Prep: 10 Minutes | Cook Time: 6 Minutes | Makes: 2 Servings

1 whole wheat crescent roll dough
4 cheese slices
1/2 cup oil
2 teaspoons garlic powder
1 teaspoon onion powder
salt, to taste
Parsley, few leaves, chopped

Unroll the dough and cut it into triangles. Place the cheese on the triangles and fold the ends. In a mixing bowl, add the oil, onion powder, garlic powder, and salt and mix it well. Spread the mixture over the crescent dough. Arrange the rolls in the air fryer basket and bake at 350°F for 6 minutes. Once the crescent rolls are baked, sprinkle parsley over them. Serve and enjoy!

Calories 787 Total Fat 76.3g Saturated Fat 19.7g Cholesterol 59mg
Sodium 563mg Total Carbohydrate 11.1g Dietary Fibre 1.8g
Total Sugars 2.7g Protein 16.4g

Morning Glory Muffins

Prep: 12 Minutes | Cook Time: 18 Minutes | Makes: 4 Servings

2 cups whole wheat flour
2 teaspoons baking powder
1 teaspoon salt
2 teaspoons cinnamon
1 teaspoon ginger
1/2 teaspoon nutmeg
¼ cup applesauce
1 cup plain yogurt
⅔ cup honey
2 teaspoons vanilla extract
1 egg
1 cup carrots
1 cup apples
½ cup raisins
½ cup pecans

Take a mixing bowl and add flour, salt, cinnamon, baking powder, nutmeg, and ginger to it. In a separate bowl mix the vanilla extract, apple sauce, yogurt, honey, and egg. Add the dry ingredients to the bowl and mix it well. Add the shredded carrots, apples, and raisins to the mixture. Place the batter in greased muffin cups and top it with pecans. Bake the muffins at 350°F for 12-18 minutes in the air fryer. Once baked, serve and enjoy!

Calories 586 Total Fat 4g Saturated Fat 1.3g Cholesterol 45mg
Sodium 668mg Total Carbohydrate 128.2g Dietary Fibre 5.7g
Total Sugars 70.8g Protein 12.8g

Carrot Raisin Muffins

Prep: 10 Minutes | Cook Time: 20 Minutes | Makes: 4 Servings

1 cup whole wheat flour
1 cup oats
2 teaspoons baking powder
salt, to taste
½ teaspoon cinnamon
¼ teaspoon nutmeg
2 eggs
1 teaspoon vanilla extract
¼ cup honey
1cup applesauce
2 cups grated carrots
½ cup raisins

Preheat the air fryer to 400°F. Take a mixing bowl and add flour, cinnamon, oats, baking powder, salt, and nutmeg to it.
Mix it together, then add eggs and honey to the mixture and whisk it well. Now, add carrots, raisins, and apple sauce to the mixture and the batter is ready. Place the batter in the greased muffin tins and bake for 20 minutes. Once baked, serve the warm muffins and enjoy!

Calories 398 Total Fat 26.8g Saturated Fat 3.6g Cholesterol 0mg
Sodium 340mg Total Carbohydrate 32.6g Dietary Fibre 10.1g
Total Sugars 7.4g Protein 9.2g

Pitta Bread Cheese Pizza

Prep: 10 Minutes | Cook Time: 6-8 Minutes | Makes: 2 Servings

2 whole wheat Pita Bread
1tablespoon Pizza Sauce
1/4 cup Mozzarella Cheese
6 pepperoni slices
1 drizzle Extra Virgin Olive Oil

Toppings:
8 slices Pepperoni
1/4 cup Sausage
1tablespoon sliced Onion
1/2 teaspoon crushed Garlic cloves

Spread the pizza sauce on the pitta bread and add toppings such as sausage, onion, garlic, pepperoni slices, along with the mozzarella cheese. Then add a few drops of oil to the pizza. Now, keep the pitta bread in the air fryer and cook for 6-8 minutes at 360°F. Once baked, slice and serve.
Enjoy!

Calories 787 Total Fat 76.3g Saturated Fat 19.7g Cholesterol 59mg
Sodium 563mg Total Carbohydrate 11.1g Dietary Fibre 1.8g
Total Sugars 2.7g Protein 16.4g

Loaded Hash Browns (GF)(DF)

Prep: 15 Minutes | Cook Time: 18 Minutes | Makes: 4 Servings

4 russet potatoes
½ cup chopped green peppers
½ cup chopped onions
2 garlic cloves
1 teaspoon paprika
salt and pepper, to taste
2 teaspoons olive oil

In a bowl, grate the potatoes and soak them in cold water for 25 minutes. Then drain off the water and pat them dry with a paper or kitchen towel. Put the potatoes back in the bowl and add onion, paprika, green pepper, olive oil, garlic, and salt and pepper. Combine the mixture well and press into large hash brown shapes. Bake in the air fryer for 18 minutes at 390°F. Serve warm and enjoy!

Calories 787 Total Fat 76.3g Saturated Fat 19.7g Cholesterol 59mg
Sodium 563mg Total Carbohydrate 11.1g Dietary Fibre 1.8g
Total Sugars 2.7g Protein 16.4g

Roasted Paprika Potatoes with Greek yogurt (GF)

Prep: 15 Minutes | Cook Time: 15 Minutes | Makes: 2 Servings

4 large sweet potatoes
2 tablespoons olive oil
1tablespoon paprika
Black pepper, to taste
2 cups Greek yogurt

Preheat the air fryer to 350°F. Cut the potato into cubes and soak it in water for 30 minutes. Then drain off and pat them dry with a paper or kitchen towel. Take a mixing bowl; add the paprika powder and half of the olive oil to it. Now, add the potatoes to the bowl and toss it well. Arrange the potatoes in the air fryer and cook for 22 minutes. Once the potato is lightly browned, sprinkle it with salt and pepper. Serve with Greek yogurt and enjoy!

Calories 318 Total Fat 9.5g Saturated Fat 2.6g Cholesterol 5mg Sodium 47mg Total Carbohydrate 46.8g Dietary Fibre 6.8g Total Sugars 5g Protein 12.6g

Air Fryer Chicken Alfredo Quinoa Balls

Prep: 15 Minutes | Cook Time: 10 Minutes | Makes: 2 Servings

7 ounces cheese
2 cups cooked quinoa
8 ounces cooked chicken
1 teaspoon garlic powder
1 teaspoon onion powder
½ teaspoon black pepper
½ teaspoon salt
1 cup Panko bread crumb
1tablespoon parsley

Prepare the cooked chicken by shredding and keeping it aside.
Take a mixing bowl and add cheese, black pepper, garlic powder, onion powder, and salt to it.
Mix it well and add quinoa and chicken to the mixture.
Now, form balls out of the mixture and coat the rolls with the Panko bread crumbs.
Arrange the balls in the air fryer and cook at 400 degrees F for 10 minutes.
Once the balls get browned, sprinkle with parsley and serve.
Enjoy!

Calories 1421 Total Fat 49.5g Saturated Fat 23.8g Cholesterol 192mg Sodium 1676mg Total Carbohydrate 151.7g Dietary Fiber 14.7g Total Sugars 4.7g   Protein 89.3g

Three Cheese Stuffed Mushrooms (GF)

Prep: 10 Minutes | Cook Time: 8 Minutes | Makes: 2 Servings

8 ounces mushrooms
4 ounces cream cheese
¼ cup parmesan cheese
1/8 cup sharp cheddar cheese
1/8 cup white cheddar cheese
1 teaspoon Worcestershire sauce
2 crushed garlic cloves
salt and pepper, to taste

Clean the mushrooms under running water and prepare the mushroom for stuffing by removing the stems. Take a mixing bowl and add Worcestershire sauce, cream cheese, Parmesan cheese, sharp Cheddar cheese, white cheese, black pepper, garlic, and salt to it. Mix it well and then stuff the cheese mixture on the mushroom caps. Now, keep the stuffed mushrooms in the air fryer and cook at 350°F for 8 minutes. Once the mushroom is cooked enough, serve and enjoy!

Calories 243 Total Fat 22.9g Saturated Fat 14.4g Cholesterol 72mg Sodium 245mg Total Carbohydrate 2.9g Dietary Fibre 0.1g Total Sugars 0.2g Protein 7.4g

Air Fried Cheesy Spinach Crostini

Prep: 10 Minutes | Cook Time: 8 Minutes | Makes: 2 Servings

1whole wheat baguette rounds
4 tablespoons of olive oil
½ cup grated Parmesan cheese
1 cup spinach dip

Slice the baguettes into rounds. Brush the baguettes rounds with olive oil. Keep the Crostini in the air fryer basket and toast for 4 minutes at 400 degrees F. Meanwhile, in a mixing bowl add the cheese and spinach dip and mix it well, Then spread the spinach dip on the Crostini and bake at 400 degrees F for 4 minutes. Serve and enjoy!

Calories 1483 Total Fat 93.6g Saturated Fat 19.9g Cholesterol 65mg Sodium 745mg Total Carbohydrate 139.4g Dietary Fiber 0g Total Sugars 8g Protein 28g

Air Fried Ricotta Fig Crostini

Prep: 10 Minutes | Cook Time: 8 Minutes | Makes: 2 Servings

6 whole wheat Baguette slices
3 Figs
4 tablespoons of Olive Oil
2 ounces Ricotta
4 Thyme sprigs, chopped

Slice the baguettes into rounds. Brush the baguettes rounds with olive oil. Keep the Crostini in the air fryer basket and toast for 4 minutes at 400°F. Meanwhile, in a mixing bowl add the cheese and spinach dip and mix it well, Then spread the spinach dip on the Crostini and bake at 400°F for 4 minutes. Serve and enjoy!

Calories 1483 Total Fat 93.6g Saturated Fat 19.9g Cholesterol 65mg Sodium 745mg Total Carbohydrate 139.4g Dietary Fibre 0g Total Sugars 8g Protein 28g

Cream Cheese Salmon with Strawberry Mint Bruschetta (GF)

Prep: 22 Minutes | Cook Time: 12 Minutes | Makes: 2 Servings

6-ounce salmon
Avocado oil spray
3 tablespoons cashew cream cheese
3 tablespoons Italian Nut crumbs

Strawberry Mint Bruschetta:
2 cups strawberries, chopped
1/4 cup Mint
2 tablespoons Olive oil
1tablespoon Celtic sea salt
1tablespoon balsamic vinegar

Brush the salmon with avocado oil spray. Then spread cream cheese on the salmon and top the salmon with nut crumbs. Place it in the air fryer and cook at 380°F for 12 minutes. Take a mixing bowl and add the diced strawberries, oil, salt, balsamic vinegar, and diced mint. Combine it well and refrigerate the mixture for 30 minutes. Once the salmon is cooked, spread on the strawberry mint bruschetta and serve. Enjoy!

Calories 391 Total Fat 29.5g Saturated Fat 6.4g Cholesterol 54mg Sodium 87mg Total Carbohydrate 14.9g Dietary Fibre 4.9g Total Sugars 7.8g Protein 20.9g

Air Fryer Bacon-Wrapped Shrimp Tapas on Avocado Toast (DF)

Prep: 20 Minutes | Cook Time: 12 Minutes | Makes: 3 Servings

24 shrimps
12 bacon slices
24 whole wheat baguette slices
1 avocado
1 lime
2 garlic cloves
2 tablespoons olive oil
salt and black pepper, to taste

Preheat the air fryer to 350°F. Slice the baguette and spray oil, salt, and pepper to it. Arrange the baguette slices in the air fryer and toast for 4 minutes. Once the slices are lightly browned, run the garlic cloves over the baguette. Meanwhile, mash the avocado with lime juice, garlic and keep it aside. Clean and pat dry the shrimp using a paper towel. Now, wrap the shrimp with a bacon slice and spray with oil on top. Arrange the shrimp in the preheated air fryer and cook at 380°F for 6 minutes. Place with avocado and sprinkle salt and pepper. Top the baguette slices with shrimps and serve. Enjoy!

Calories 179 Total Fat 2.7g Saturated Fat 0.4g Cholesterol 0mg Sodium 14mg Total Carbohydrate 36.2g Dietary Fibre 5.9g Total Sugars 3.4g Protein 4g

Perfect Crostini

Prep: 20 Minutes | Cook Time: 15 Minutes | Makes: 2 Servings

Half a baguette
2 tablespoons of Olive oil
1 garlic clove
120 grams ricotta cheese
1tablespoon basil
1 red chili
100 grams black olives
1 tomato

Preheat the air fryer to 2400°F for a few minutes Cut the baguette into slices and brush it with oil. Arrange the slices in the air fryer and bake for 15 minutes. Once the crostini is baked, rub it with garlic clove. Meanwhile, take a mixing bowl and add cheese, olives, and chilli. Then add salt and pepper to the bowl. Spread the mixture on crostini and top with tomato slices and drizzle with a few drops of oil. Serve and enjoy!

Calories 324 Total Fat 24.4g Saturated Fat 5.7g Cholesterol 19mg Sodium 628mg Total Carbohydrate 19.1g Dietary Fibre 2.6g Total Sugars 1.6g Protein 9.7g

Cannoli Stuffed & French Toast

Prep: 20Minutes | Cook Time: 12Minutes | Makes: 2 Servings

Cannoli Filling:
1 cup ricotta cheese
2 tablespoons powdered sugar
1/2 teaspoon vanilla extract
3 tablespoons mini chocolate chips

French toast:
4 slices brioche bread
2 eggs
2 tablespoons butter melted
1 cup half & half
2 tablespoons sugar
2 teaspoons vanilla extract
½ teaspoon cinnamon
Maple syrup

Take a mixing bowl and add ricotta cheese and sugar to it.
Mix it well. Then add the vanilla extract and chocolate chips to the bowl and keep them aside. Preheat the air fryer at 350°F for 5 minutes. Grease the air fryer basket with cooking spray.
Add the eggs and butter to the bowl and whisk well. Then add cinnamon, milk and cream, sugar, and vanilla extract and mix together. Soak the bread slice in the mixture and place it in the greased air fryer basket. Place the ricotta cheese mixture on the bread slice and repeat the same process for the remaining bread slices. Bake the bread slice for 10-12 minutes by flipping halfway through cooking. Once baked, top the bread with maple syrup. Serve and enjoy!

Calories 886 Total Fat 44.7g Saturated Fat 19.1g Cholesterol 247mg Sodium 383mg Total Carbohydrate 89.9g Dietary Fibre 1.3g Total Sugars 31.8g Protein 33.4g

Greek Smashed Potatoes (GF)(DF)

Prep: 20 Minutes | Cook Time: 40 Minutes | Makes: 4 Servings

2 pounds small potatoes
¼ cup olive oil
1 teaspoon oregano dried
1 lemon zest
salt & pepper, to taste

Preheat the air fryer to 350°F. Clean the potatoes and boil them for 15 minutes. Then drain the potatoes using a colander. Meanwhile, take a mixing bowl and add zest, salt, pepper, oregano, and olive oil and mix it well. Now, toss the potatoes in the oregano mixture and place the potatoes in the baking tray. Flatten the potatoes using a masher and roast the potatoes for 40 minutes. Once the potatoes are crispy, serve warm and enjoy!

Calories 273 Total Fat 13.2g Saturated Fat 1.9g Cholesterol 0mg Sodium 28mg Total Carbohydrate 37.1g Dietary Fibre 5.9g 21% Total Sugars 3.1g   Protein 4g

Greek Style Lemon Potatoes (GF)(DF)

Prep: 20 Minutes | Cook Time: 40 Minutes | Makes: 4Servings

2 pounds small potatoes
¼ cup olive oil
1 teaspoon oregano dried
1 lemon zest
salt & pepper, to taste

Wash the potatoes, dry them and chop them into wedges. Take a mixing bowl and add salt, lime juice, oregano, olive oil and mix it well. Then add the potatoes to the bowl and toss it well. Preheat the air fryer for 3 minutes at 400°F. Arrange the potatoes in the air fryer and cook for 22 minutes at 380°F. Flip the potatoes and cook for 10 minutes. Once baked, drizzle lemon juice over the potatoes and enjoy.

Calories 310 Total Fat 17.5g Saturated Fat 3g Cholesterol 0mg Sodium 658mg Total Carbohydrate 39.1g 1 Dietary Fibre 3.4g Total Sugars 0.8g Protein 4.3g

Greek Feta Fries in an Air-Fryer(GF)

Prep: 25 Minutes | Cook Time: 17 Minutes | Makes: 2 Servings

Cooking spray
 2 Yukon Gold potatoes
1 tablespoon olive oil
2 teaspoons lemon zest
1/2 teaspoon oregano
1/2 teaspoon kosher salt
1/4 teaspoon garlic powder
1/4 teaspoon onion powder
1/4 teaspoon paprika powder
1/2 teaspoon black pepper
 1/2 cup feta cheese
2 ounces shredded chicken breast
1/4 cup Tzatziki
1/4 cup plum tomato
 2 tablespoons chopped red onion
1 tablespoon parsley
1 tablespoon oregano

Preheat the air fryer to 400°F. Grease the air fryer basket with cooking spray. Cut the potatoes into quarter-inch fries.
Meanwhile, take a bowl and add lemon zest, oregano, onion powder, salt, garlic powder, paprika, and pepper to it.
Toss the potatoes in the bowl by adding oil.
Place the potatoes in the air fryer and cook for 17 minutes.
Once the potatoes become crisp, top the potatoes with cheese, chicken pieces, tomato, tzatziki, onion, oregano, parsley.
Serve and enjoy!

Calories 606Total Fat 38g Saturated Fat 13.7g Cholesterol 83mg
Sodium 2266mg Total Carbohydrate 49.8g 1 Dietary Fibre 3.2g
Total Sugars 4.8g   Protein 20.8g

Air Fryer Chicken with Quinoa Salad

Prep: 20 Minutes | Cook Time: 35-45 Minutes | Makes: 2 Servings

1 cup quinoa
2 teaspoons of olive oil
2 teaspoons cumin powder
2 teaspoons coriander powder
2 teaspoons paprika powder
2 chicken breast fillets
100 grams thawed broad beans
2 medium tomatoes
4 spring onions
120g Kale & Baby Spinach
1/2 cup mint leaves
1/4 cup chopped almonds
1/2 cup Yogurt
2 tablespoons lemon juice
1tablespoontahini
1 garlic clove

Put the rinsed quinoa in the pan and then add 240ml water and cook it over high heat for 10 minutes. Once the quinoa is cooked, keep the grains aside to cool. Preheat the air fryer to 400°F.
 Meanwhile, add cumin, paprika, and coriander to a bowl and toss the chicken in the mixture. Drizzle the chicken with oil and arrange the chicken in the air fryer and cook for 15 minutes. When the chicken is cooked enough, keep them aside. Now, cook the beans in the pan by adding water for 2 minutes. Once the beans are lightly cooked, take a mixing bowl and add the beans with quinoa, tomato, kale, spring onion, almonds, spinach, and mint to it.
Combine the lemon juice, yogurt, tahini, and garlic in a bowl.
Then add the lemon juice mixture to the quinoa and serve it with chicken. Enjoy!

Calories 1483 Total Fat 93.6g Saturated Fat 19.9g Cholesterol 65mg
Sodium 745mg Total Carbohydrate 139.4g Dietary Fibre 0g Total Sugars 8g
Protein 28g

Buffalo Quinoa Bites

Prep: 10 Minutes | Cook Time: 7 Minutes | Makes: 4 Servings

2 cups cooked quinoa
1 cup cannellini beans
1 cup Panko
1 egg
1/2 cup buffalo wing sauce
salt and pepper, to taste
2 ounces crumbled cheese

Take a mixing bowl and add quinoa, egg, salt, pepper, mashed cannellini beans, breadcrumbs, and buffalo sauce to it.
Now form 16 balls out of the mixture.
Flatten the balls and add little cheese on the center and seal the balls.
Arrange the balls in the air fryer at 204°C (400°F) for 7 minutes.
Flip the balls halfway through cooking.
Once the balls are cooked enough, toss it with buffalo wing sauce.
Serve and enjoy!

Calories 646 Total Fat 12.8g Saturated Fat 4.3g Cholesterol 56mg Sodium 364mg Total Carbohydrate 102g Dietary Fibre 18.6g Total Sugars 2.9g Protein 31.4g

Tofu Coated with Quinoa Flakes

Prep: 15 Minutes | Cook Time: 10 Minutes | Makes: 2 Servings

1 block tofu, cubed
1/2 cup cornstarch
1/2 cup unsweetened soy milk
1/2 cup quinoa flakes
1/2 cup nutritional yeast
1tablespoon oregano
1tablespoon parsley
1tablespoon sage leaves
2tablespoons rosemary
1 teaspoon black pepper

Preheat the air fryer to 400°F. Place the cornstarch in a bowl and the soy milk in another bowl. Then combine the quinoa flakes, sage, rosemary, salt nutritional yeast, oregano, and pepper in a large bowl. Slice the tofu into pieces and coat the tofu in cornstarch first in the soy milk. Then dip the tofu in the quinoa mixture and place it on the air fryer basket. Cook the tofu for 10 minutes, Once the tofu becomes browned, serve warm and enjoy!

Calories 452 Total Fat 7.6g Saturated Fat 1.2g Cholesterol 0mg Sodium 69mg Total Carbohydrate 74.6g 27% Dietary Fibre 16.1g Total Sugars 4.4g Protein 28.1g

Air Fryer Zucchini Fries With Tzatziki Dip

Prep: 15 Minutes | Cook Time: 10 Minutes | Makes: 2 Servings

1 Zucchini
1 Cup Oat Bran
1 Cup Baking Flour
2 Eggs beaten
Garlic
Salt & Pepper

Tzatziki Dip:
4 tablespoons Greek Yogurt
1 Cucumber
1 Lemon juice
Mint
Dill

Take 3 bowls; egg mixture in one bowl, baking flour in second and oat bran in the third bowl. Add salt and pepper to the oat bran bowl. Thinly slice the courgette and coat them in the baking flour, and egg mixture and then in the oat bran. Arrange the courgette in the air fryer and cook at 204°C (400°F) for 10 minutes. Meanwhile, you can prepare the tzatziki dip by mixing all the ingredients under the tzatziki dip in the list. Serve the courgette fries with dip. Enjoy!

Calories 511 Total Fat 17.2g Saturated Fat 7.1g Cholesterol 164mg Sodium 705mg Total Carbohydrate 68g Dietary Fibre 7.4g Total Sugars 11.8g Protein 23.7g

Air Fryer Pitta Pockets (DF)

Prep: 10 Minutes | Cook Time: 7 Minutes | Makes: 3 Servings

3 pita pockets
2 tablespoons olive oil
1 teaspoon salt
1 teaspoon pepper
½ teaspoon garlic powder
½ teaspoon parsley

Make triangles from the pitta pockets.
Take a mixing bowl and add oil, pepper, garlic powder, salt, and parsley to a bowl.
Add oil, herbs to the triangles and toss it well.
Arrange the pitta triangles in the air fryer and bake at 177°C (350°F), for 7 minutes.
Once baked, serve and enjoy!

Calories 225 Total Fat 9.8g Saturated Fat 1.3g Cholesterol 0mg
Sodium 1007mg Total Carbohydrate 29.8g Dietary Fibre 1.6g
Total Sugars 0.8g Protein 4.8g

Air Fryer feta cheese Appetizer

Prep: 15 Minutes | Cook Time: 10 Minutes | Makes: 2 Servings

1 2/3 grams feta cheese
2 tablespoons olive oil
2 tablespoons honey
1 teaspoon dried oregano
1teaspoon chili flakes

Preheat the air fryer to 400°F. Add oil, honey, over the feta cheese. Now, spread dried oregano and chilli flakes and cook for 10 minutes. Once the cheese starts melting, serve and enjoy!

Calories 516 Total Fat 40.7g Saturated Fat 20.7g Cholesterol 111mg
Sodium 1396mg Total Carbohydrate 22.9g Dietary Fibre 0.4g
Total Sugars 22.4g Protein 17.9g

Air-Fryer White Fish Cakes

Prep: 18 Minutes | Cook Time: 10 Minutes | Makes: 2 Servings

Cooking spray

12 ounces white fish
1/3 cup wheat Panko bread crumbs
3 tablespoons cilantro
2 tablespoons Thai sweet chili sauce
2tablespoons canola mayonnaise
2 eggs
salt and black pepper, to taste
2 lime wedges

Grease the air fryer basket with oil or cooking spray. Take a mixing bowl and add fish, breadcrumbs, egg, salt, cilantro, chilli sauce, mayonnaise, and pepper to it. Make cake from the mixture and brush oil on the cakes. Arrange the fish cakes in the air fryer basket and cook at 400°F for 10 minutes. Once fish cakes are cooked, serve with lime wedges.
Enjoy!

Calories 443 Total Fat 20.6g Saturated Fat 3.2g Cholesterol 240mg
Sodium 904mg Total Carbohydrate 16.8g Dietary Fibre 2.3g
Total Sugars 7.7g Protein 46.7g

Air Fryer Olives, Garlic & Tomatoes

Prep: 15 Minutes | Cook Time: 5 Minutes | Makes: 2 Servings

1 Cup Kalamata olives
1 Cup green olives
1Cup grape tomatoes
1/4 cup garlic cloves
2 tablespoons olive oil
2 tablespoons herbs de Provence

Take a mixing bowl and add garlic, olives, tomatoes, and olive oil to it. Add the herbs and place the mixture in the air fryer basket for 5 minutes at 360°F. Once it becomes golden, toss the mixture with cooked pasta.Serve and enjoy!

Calories 242 Total Fat 21.7g Saturated Fat 3g Cholesterol 0mg
Sodium 631mg Total Carbohydrate 13.6g Dietary Fibre 3.7g
Total Sugars 2.5g Protein 2.5g

VEGETABLE RECIPES

Coated Wedges in the Air Fryer (DF)

Prep: 15 Minutes | Cook Time: 2 Minutes | Makes: 2 Servings

3 potatoes cut into wedges
3 tablespoons of olive oil
2 teaspoons chopped cilantro
2 tablespoons corn flour
½ teaspoon garlic
 Salt and black pepper, to taste
Oil spray , for greasing

Take a bowl and add water, ice cubes, and salt to it. Then put the potato wedges in it and wait for 30 minutes. Dry them using a paper towel. Meanwhile, take a bowl and add garlic, salt, pepper, olive oil, cilantro, and cornflour to it. Combine the mixture well and add the wedges to the bowl; toss it well. Arrange the wedges in the air fryer and cook at 400°F for 20 minutes.
Once it is cooked, serve and enjoy!

Calories 431 Total Fat 21.9g Saturated Fat 3.2g Cholesterol 0mg
Sodium 20mg Total Carbohydrate 56.1g Dietary Fibre 8.2g
Total Sugars 3.7g Protein 5.9g

Air Fryer Spanish Spicy Potatoes(DF)

Prep: 15 Minutes | Cook Time: 20 Minutes | Makes: 2 Servings

4 potatoes
1 tablespoon extra virgin olive oil
2 teaspoons paprika
2 teaspoons dried garlic
1 teaspoon Barbacoa seasoning
salt & pepper

Sauce ingredients:
1diced onion
1/2 cup tomato sauce
1 tomato
1 tablespoon red wine vinegar
1 teaspoon paprika
1 teaspoon chili powder
2 teaspoons coriander
2 teaspoons thyme
2 teaspoons mixed spice
1 teaspoon oregano
1 teaspoon rosemary

Cut the potato into wedges and put them in the bowl; add all the seasonings and oil to it. Toss it well and place them in the air fryer. Cook at 400°F for 20 minutes. Shake the potatoes halfway to cooking. Meanwhile, prepare the spicy sauce by combining the ingredients. Serve the potatoes with sauce and enjoy!

Calories 419 Total Fat 8.4g Saturated Fat 1.3g Cholesterol 0mg Sodium 418mg Total Carbohydrate 81g Dietary Fibre 15g Total Sugars 11.1g   Protein 9.7g

Air Fryer Spicy Potato Wedges (GF) (DF)

Prep: 15 Minutes | Cook Time: 30 Minutes | Makes: 2 Servings

2 pounds russet potatoes
Cooking spray
2 tablespoons vegetable oil
1 teaspoon chili powder
1 teaspoon cumin powder
½ teaspoon paprika powder
½ teaspoon coriander powder
½ teaspoon garlic powder
¼ teaspoon cinnamon powder
salt , to taste

Chop the potatoes into wedges and rinse them in the water. Pat dry the potatoes using a kitchen or paper towel. Preheat the air fryer to 400°F and grease the air fryer basket with oil. Take a mixing bowl and add all the spice powders to it and then add oil; toss the potatoes in the bowl mixture. Place the potatoes in the air fryer basket and cook for 25-30 minutes. Once the potatoes become crispy, serve and enjoy!

Calories 444 Total Fat 14.8g Saturated Fat 2.9g Cholesterol 0mg Sodium 120mg Total Carbohydrate 72.4g Dietary Fibre 11.4g Total Sugars 5.3g Protein 8g

Spanish Spinach Croquettes

Prep: 15 Minutes | Cook Time: 10 Minutes | Makes: 2 Servings

1 cup almond milk
1 cup grams spinach
½ cup vegetable stock
2 cups breadcrumbs
2 onions
salt and black pepper, to taste
4 garlic cloves
1/2 cup tapioca flour
3 tablespoons olive oil
1 cup coriander leaves

Take a pan and add 480ml of water and bring it to boil. Then add the spinach to the pan and then cook for 3 minutes. Once cooked, strain the water and keep them aside. Now, add the almond milk, vegetable stock to the pan and then boil for 4 minutes. Add oil to the pan over medium heat and sauté garlic for a minute. Then add the onions and cook for a few minutes. Meanwhile, add the flour to the pan and then mix everything. Mix the chopped spinach and coriander in the pan. Season it with salt and pepper. Transfer the mixture into the bowl and refrigerate for a few hours. Now, make the croquettes and soak them in the almond milk, then breadcrumbs. Place the croquettes in the greased air fryer and cook at 360°F for 10 minutes. Once baked, serve the croquettes with ketchup. Serve and enjoy!

Calories 106 Total Fat 56g Saturated Fat 29.8g Cholesterol 0mg Sodium 931mg Total Carbohydrate 124.5g Dietary Fibre 13.4g Total Sugars 16.2g Protein 22.6g

Roasted Savory Carrots (GF)

Prep: 18 Minutes | Cook Time: 20 Minutes | Makes: 2 Servings

1 cup carrots
2 tablespoons olive oil
½ teaspoon garlic powder
½ teaspoon paprika
1/4 cup parmesan cheese
salt and black pepper, to taste

Clean and peel the carrots. Put the carrots in the bowl and add oil, paprika powder, and garlic powder. Arrange the carrots in the air fryer basket and cook for 20 minutes at 380°F. Once cooked, top the carrots with Parmesan cheese. Sprinkle salt and pepper into the carrots and serve. Enjoy!

Calories 158 Total Fat 14.8g Saturated Fat 2.5g Cholesterol 3mg Sodium 71mg Total Carbohydrate 6.4g Dietary Fibre 1.6g Total Sugars 2.9g Protein 1.8g

Smoky Cauliflower (GF)

Prep: 18 Minutes | Cook Time: 10 Minutes | Makes: 2 Servings

1 cauliflower cut into florets
2 tablespoons olive oil
1 teaspoon smoked paprika
3/4 teaspoon salt
2 garlic cloves, minced
2 tablespoons parsley

Take a mixing bowl and add oil, minced garlic, salt, and paprika. Add the cauliflower florets to the bowl and toss it well. Then place the florets in the air fryer basket that is greased with oil spray, and cook for 10 minutes at 450 degrees F. Once the cauliflower is cooked, sprinkle with parsley. Serve and enjoy!

Calories 141 Total Fat 14.2g Saturated Fat 2g Cholesterol 0mg Sodium 890mg Total Carbohydrate 4.5g Dietary Fiber 1.8g Total Sugars 1.4g Protein 1.4g

Garlic Parmesan Air Fryer Roasted Radishes(GF)

Prep: 15 Minutes | Cook Time: 10 Minutes | Makes: 2 Servings

10-ounces Radishes
1 tablespoon Olive Oil
1 Garlic clove
Pinch of Kosher Salt
2 tablespoons Parmesan cheese
Red pepper flakes

Chop the radishes into quarters and add oil to them. Place the radish in the air fryer basket and cook at 350 degrees F for 8 minutes. Meanwhile, take a mixing bowl and add oil, garlic, salt, and pepper flakes. Mix it well. Once the radishes are cooked, toss them in the olive oil mixture and add grated cheese. Then place the radish in the air fryer basket and cook for 6 minutes at 400 degrees F. Once the radish becomes golden brown, serve and enjoy!

Calories 178 Total Fat 13.3g Saturated Fat 5.1g Cholesterol 20mg Sodium 393mg Total Carbohydrate 6.8g Dietary Fibre 2.5g Total Sugars 2.8g Protein 10.2g

Air Fryer Spinach (GF)

Prep: 15 Minutes | Cook Time: 5 Minutes | Makes: 2 Servings

1 cup Spinach
4 Teaspoons Butter
2 Teaspoons Garlic Powder
Salt & Pepper, to taste

Clean the spinach under running water. Then place the spinach in the air fryer basket and add butter, salt, garlic powder. Cook for 5 minutes at 400 degrees F. Once cooked, serve, and enjoy!

Calories 80 Total Fat 7.7g Saturated Fat 4.8g Cholesterol 20mg Sodium 67mg Total Carbohydrate 2.6g Dietary Fiber 0.6g Total Sugars 0.8g Protein 1g

Orange-Cranberry Butternut Squash with Ginger(GF)

Prep: 18 Minutes | Cook Time: 10 Minutes | Makes: 2 Servings

2 pounds butternut squash
½ cup cranberries
½ cup orange juice
¼ cup honey
¼ cup butter
2 tablespoons grated ginger
salt, to taste
⅛ Teaspoon white pepper
½ sliced orange
1 tablespoon parsley

Place the aluminium foil in the air fryer basket. Slice the butternut squash and place it in the air fryer basket and top it with cranberries. Meanwhile, take a mixing bowl and add grated ginger, juice, honey, melted butter, salt, and pepper to it. Mix it well.
Then pour the mixture over the squash and cook at 177°C 350°F for 10 minutes. Cook for 4 more minutes until the squash gets browned. Once browned, serve the squash with an orange slice and parsley. Serve and enjoy!

Calories 141 Total Fat 14.2g Saturated Fat 2g Cholesterol 0mg Sodium 890mg Total Carbohydrate 4.5g Dietary Fiber 1.8g Total Sugars 1.4g Protein 1.4g

Air Fryer Garlic Aioli Artichokes (GF)

Prep: 20 Minutes | Cook Time: 8 Minutes | Makes: 2 Servings

12 ounces artichoke hearts
2 tablespoons olive oil
2 tablespoons Parmesan cheese
½ teaspoon Italian seasoning
½ teaspoon kosher salt
½ teaspoon lemon pepper
½ teaspoon garlic powder

Garlic Aioli:
1/2 cup mayonnaise
2 garlic cloves
1tablespoon lemon juice
1/2 teaspoon kosher salt
1/4 teaspoon black pepper

Put all the garlic aioli ingredients in the bowl and mix it well. Refrigerate the mixture for 30 minutes. Preheat the air fryer to 400 degrees F. Drain and pat dry the quartered artichoke hearts. Put the artichoke in the bowl and toss it well with all the remaining listed ingredients. Keep the artichokes in the air fryer and cook for 8 minutes. Cook the artichoke hearts until crispy and brown. Serve it with garlic aioli sauce and enjoy!

Calories 297 Total Fat 20.6g Saturated Fat 6.1g Cholesterol 21mg Sodium 1002mg Total Carbohydrate 19.9g Dietary Fiber 9.4g Total Sugars 2g Protein 14.7g

Herb Air Fryer Butternut Squash(GF)

Prep: 10 Minutes | Cook Time: 16 Minutes | Makes: 2 Servings

1 pound butternut squash
2 tablespoons extra virgin olive oil
3/4 teaspoon Pink Salt
1 teaspoon Garlic Powder
2 teaspoons Italian Seasoning

Cut the butter squash into cubes and add oil, garlic powder, salt, and Italian seasoning to it. Toss it well and keep it aside. Preheat the air fryer to 400 degrees F. Place the butter squash in the air fryer and cook for 8 minutes. Flip the squash halfway through cooking and cook for another 8 minutes. Once it becomes crispy, serve warm and enjoy!

Calories 285 Total Fat 17.6g Saturated Fat 2.8g Cholesterol 21mg Sodium 35mg Total Carbohydrate 28g Dietary Fibre 4.7g Total Sugars 5.7g Protein 8.8g

Air Fryer Curried Carrots with Dates & Almonds (GF)

Prep: 12 Minutes | Cook Time: 25 Minutes | Makes: 2 Servings

1/3 cup almonds
4 carrots
2 teaspoons avocado oil
1 teaspoon curry powder
salt and black pepper, to taste
4 dates
2 tablespoons Extra Virgin Olive Oil
2 tablespoons of Lemon juice

Preheat the air fryer to 350 degrees F. Place the almonds on the baking sheet and roast them for 10 minutes. Meanwhile, add the carrots coins, curry powder, salt, avocado oil, pepper to the bowl and mix it well. Place the carrots in the air fryer and cook for 15 minutes at 390 degrees F. Put the carrots to the dish and top with roasted almonds and dates. Sprinkle olive oil and lemon juice into it. Serve and enjoy!

Calories 141 Total Fat 14.2g Saturated Fat 2g Cholesterol 0mg Sodium 890mg Total Carbohydrate 4.5g Dietary Fiber 1.8g Total Sugars 1.4g Protein 1.4g

Air Fryer Vegetable Kabobs(GF)

Prep: 12 Minutes | Cook Time: 10 Minutes | Makes: 2 Servings

1 cup button mushrooms, cubed
1 cup cherry tomatoes, cubed
1 zucchini, cubed
1/2 teaspoon cumin
1/2 sliced bell pepper, cubed
1 onion, cubed
Salt, to taste

Preheat the air fryer to 400°F. Place the veggies on the skewers. Sprinkle cumin and salt over the top. Toast the veggies on the skewer for 10 minutes and turn the skewer stand in the air fryer. Once cooked, serve the veggie kabobs and enjoy!

Calories 73 Total Fat 0.7g Saturated Fat 0.1g Cholesterol 0mg Sodium 98mg Total Carbohydrate 15.6g Dietary Fibre 4.2g Total Sugars 8.5g Protein 4.1g

Air Fryer Pineapple Teriyaki Veggie Kabobs(DF)

Prep: 10 Minutes | Cook Time: 12 Minutes | Makes: 2 Servings

4 Pineapple Chunks
Salt and black pepper, to taste
4 Vegetable Kabobs
½ cup Teriyaki Sauce

Place the pineapple pieces in the skewer alternative to vegetable kabobs. Fix the skewer in the air fryer rack and spread teriyaki sauce. Season the chunks with salt and pepper. Cook the pineapple chunks for a few minutes. Once done, serve it with teriyaki sauce and enjoy!

Calories 688 Total Fat 34.4g Saturated Fat 0g Cholesterol 0mg Sodium 2764mg Total Carbohydrate 60.5g Dietary Fibre 4.7g Total Sugars 42.7g Protein 58.1g

Mixed Veggies (GF)

Prep: 10 Minutes | Cook Time: 20 Minutes | Makes: 15 Servings

2 cups carrots
2 cups potatoes
2 cups shallots
2 cups zucchini
2 cups yellow squash
Salt and black pepper
1 tablespoon Italian seasoning
2 tablespoons ranch seasoning
4 tablespoons olive oil

Cut all the veggies into cubes and place them in the bowl and add the seasoning to it. Toss it well and keep it in the greased air fryer basket. Cook the veggies at 356 degrees F for 20 minutes. Serve and enjoy!

Calories 78 Total Fat 4.1g Saturated Fat 0.6g Cholesterol 1mg Sodium 107mg Total Carbohydrate 9g Dietary Fiber 1.1g Total Sugars 1.4g Protein 1.3g

Mediterranean Vegetable Medley(GF) (DF)

Prep: 20 Minutes | Cook Time: 10Minutes | Makes: Servings

1 eggplant, cubed
1 zucchini, cubed
1 summer squash, cubed
1 cup shiitake mushrooms, cubed
1 cup whole grape tomatoes, cubed
2 tablespoons olive oil
2 cloves garlic
½ teaspoon dried oregano
½ teaspoon kosher salt
1 teaspoon lemon zest
1 teaspoon of lemon juice

Clean and slice all the veggies. Take a mixing bowl and add eggplant, zucchini, olive oil, garlic, summer squash, mushrooms, tomatoes oregano, and salt to it. Mix it well and arrange the veggies in the air fryer basket. Cook for 10 minutes at 360 degrees F.
Once the veggies are browned, drizzle with lemon zest and juice. Then serve. Enjoy!

Calories 267 Total Fat 15.2g Saturated Fat 2.2g Cholesterol 0mg Sodium 777mg Total Carbohydrate 34.2g Dietary Fiber 12.7g Total Sugars 16g Protein 6.3g

Roasted Vegetables(GF) (DF)

Prep: 10 Minutes | Cook Time: 15 Minutes | Makes: 2Servings

Firm veggies:
1 sweet potato
1 potato
1 cup butternut squash
1 carrot

Other Veggies:
1/2 head broccoli
1 red onion

Seasoning:
3 tablespoons olive oil
1 teaspoon kosher salt

Clean and peel the firm veggies and cut them into chunks. Preheat the air fryer to 350 degrees F. Drain the veggies and pat dry them. Take a mixing bowl and add oil, salt seasonings to the bowl and toss them with the firm veggies. Keep the veggies in the air fryer and fry for 5 minutes. Meanwhile, mix the other veggies with the oil and salt and mix it well. Then add the remaining veggies to the air fryer and cook for another 5 minutes. Once all the veggies are cooked, serve and enjoy!

Calories 688 Total Fat 34.4g Saturated Fat 0g Cholesterol 0mg Sodium 2764mg Total Carbohydrate 60.5g Dietary Fibre 4.7g Total Sugars 42.7g Protein 58.1g

Air Fryer Roasted Vegetables With Halloumi Cheese(GF)

Prep: 20Minutes | Cook Time: 18 Minutes | Makes: 2 Servings

1 onion wedges
1 sliced red pepper sliced
2 sliced courgettes
1tablespoon Extra Virgin Olive Oil
6 cherry tomatoes
1 block sliced halloumi cheese

Add the onion, peppers, and courgettes to the air fryer basket and toss it with oil. Cook at 400 degrees F for 10 minutes. Then add salt and pepper to the veggies and add the cherry tomatoes Continue cooking the veggies for 5 minutes. Then add halloumi slices and cook for 3 minutes at 392 degrees F.
Serve and enjoy!

Calories 198 Total Fat 10.5g Saturated Fat 1.8g Cholesterol 0mg Sodium 88mg Total Carbohydrate 22.9g Dietary Fiber 6.7g Total Sugars 14.7g Protein 8.2g

Roast Mix Vegetables & Feta (GF)

Prep: 12 Minutes | Cook Time: 15 Minutes | Makes: 2 Servings

½ sliced eggplant
1 quartered zucchini
1 sliced red pepper
1 yellow pepper
1 chopped red onion
4 cloves garlic
½ teaspoon paprika
1 teaspoon mixed herbs
salt and black pepper, to taste
3 tablespoons olive oil
Crumbled feta
Parsley , as needed

Chop all the veggies and toss them with olive oil and seasoning in the mixing bowl. Preheat the air fryer at 366 degrees F. Place the veggies in the air fryer basket and cook for 15 minutes and add the tomatoes halfway through cooking. Once the veggies are browned enough, transfer them t the bowl. Season the veggies with fresh herbs and cheese and serve. Enjoy!

Calories 326 Total Fat 23.8g Saturated Fat 4.4g Cholesterol 8mg Sodium 117mg Total Carbohydrate 28.7g Dietary Fiber 8.6g Total Sugars 11g Protein 6.3g

Briam Greek Roasted Vegetables

Prep: 20 Minutes | Cook Time: 22 Minutes | Makes: 2 Servings

1 sliced potato
1 eggplant round
1 zucchini rounds
1 red onion circle
1 large tomato rounds
1cup extra virgin olive oil
1 cloves garlic
1 teaspoon oregano
salt and black pepper, to taste
1 can diced tomatoes
2 sprigs thyme

Topping :
½ cup Feta cheese
3 slices Crusty whole wheat bread
few olives

Clean and slice the veggies; take a mixing bowl and add the veggies and add oil, garlic, pepper, salt, and oregano to it. Toss it well and add the diced tomatoes and half a cup of water to it. Foil the dish and place it in the preheated air fryer and cook for 22 minutes at 390 degrees F. Once the veggies get browned, serve the veggies with thyme, cheese, olives, and crusty bread.

Calories 1144 Total Fat 103.2g Saturated Fat 14.9g Cholesterol 0mg Sodium 552mg Total Carbohydrate 57.5g Dietary Fiber 11.5g Total Sugars 15.3g Protein 11.2g

Grilled Veggies & Couscous

Prep: 10 Minutes | Cook Time: 15 Minutes | Makes: 2 Servings

1 zucchini
1 paprika
1/2 cup mushrooms
1/2 cup shrimp
salt and black pepper, to taste
2 teaspoons Italian herbs
½ cup couscous
½ cup water
4 tablespoons cheese

Chop the zucchini and mushrooms, and sprinkle paprika on them. Place them in the bowl and add Italian herbs, salt, and pepper to it. Toss it well and bake the veggies in the air fryer at 400°F for 6 minutes. Meanwhile, boil the water in the pan by adding little salt. Then add couscous to the water and leave them in the pan. Now, add shrimp to the veggies l and continue cooking for 2 minutes. Once cooked, toss the veggies and shrimp with cheese and serve. Enjoy!

Calories 391 Total Fat 8.9g Saturated Fat 3.8g Cholesterol 84mg Sodium 756mg Total Carbohydrate 62.7g Dietary Fiber 18.8g Total Sugars 2.2g Protein 29.5g

Crispy Air Fryer Chickpeas(GF) (DF)

Prep: 12 Minutes | Cook Time: 15 Minutes | Makes: 2Servings

20 ounces can of chickpeas
1 tablespoon olive oil
1 teaspoon salt
1/2 teaspoon garlic powder
1/4 teaspoon onion powder
1/2 teaspoon paprika

Preheat the air fryer to 400 degrees F. Take a mixing bowl and add chickpeas, oil, and spices to it and toss well. Place the chickpeas in the air fryer basket and cook for 15 minutes. Once the chickpeas become crispy, add salt and pepper to them. Serve and enjoy!

Calories 402 Total Fat 10.3g Saturated Fat 1.3g Cholesterol 0mg Sodium 2011mg Total Carbohydrate 65.2g Dietary Fiber 12.8g Total Sugars 0.3g Protein 14.3g

Garlic and Herb Roasted Chickpeas(DF)

Prep: 12 Minutes | Cook Time: 15 Minutes | Makes: 2Servings

3 cans chickpeas
1 tablespoon olive oil
2 tablespoons nutritional
yeast
2 teaspoons garlic powder
2 tablespoons mixed herbs
Salt and black pepper, to taste

Rinse and drain the chickpeas and place them in the mixing bowl by adding a few drops of oil. Then add the seasonings to the bowl and mix it well. Once the chickpeas get coated with the mixture, place the chickpeas in the air fryer basket Fry the chickpeas at 400 degrees F for 15 minutes. Stir the chickpeas halfway through cooking. When the chickpeas get browned, serve warm and enjoy!

Calories 600 Total Fat 12.9g Saturated Fat 1.5g Cholesterol 0mg Sodium 40mg Total Carbohydrate 94.7g Dietary Fiber 27.8g Total Sugars 16.4g Protein 31.6g

Air Fryer Black Eyed Peas & Greens(GF)

Prep: 12 Minutes | Cook Time: 10 Minutes | Makes: 2servings

14 cup black-eyed peas
2 cups collard greens
1 tablespoon chili powder
1 tablespoon seasoning salt
2 tablespoons garlic powder
2 tablespoons olive oil

Drain and rinse the black-eyed peas and add them to the mixing bowl. Now, add chili powder, salt, and pepper to the mixing bowl and toss it with peas. Place the peas in the air fryer basket and fry at 350 degrees F for 5 minutes. Meanwhile, take a bowl and add oil and toss the greens. Stir the peas halfway through cooking and add the greens on top of the peas. Continue to cook for 5 more minutes. Once cooked, serve, and enjoy!

Calories 1432 Total Fat 28.6g Saturated Fat 2.1g Cholesterol 0mg Sodium 3886mg Total Carbohydrate 235g Dietary Fiber 59.7g Total Sugars 2.3g Protein 86.2g

Air Fryer Black-Eyed Pea Dumpling Stew(GF)

Prep: 12 Minutes | Cook Time: 25 Minutes | Makes: 2Servings

2 white potatoes
2 onions
2 tomatoes
1 eggplant
3 carrots
1 sweet potato
1 hot pepper
1 bay leaf
salt and black pepper to taste
4 cups water

Ingredients for Dumplings:
2 cups dry black-eyed peas
1/4 cup flour
1tablespoonparsley flakes
1 cup vegetable broth
1/6 teaspoon salt

Add all the ingredients for stew in a large pot and cook for 20 minutes until tender. Next add peas, flour, salt, parsley, and little water to the food processor. Pulse until the dough gets formed. Make balls from the dough and put the balls in the air fryer basket. Spray the balls with oil and cook for 10 minutes.
Add it to stew and serve hot.

Calories 437 Total Fat 2g Saturated Fat 0.3g Cholesterol 0mg Sodium 702mg Total Carbohydrate 96.3g Dietary Fibre 21.8g Total Sugars 25.8g Protein 14.1g

Garlicky Couscous

Prep: 12 Minutes | Cook Time: 25 Minutes | Makes: 2 Servings

2 tablespoons butter
1 garlic cloves
2 cups couscous
1.5 cups chicken broth
1/4 cup Parmesan Cheese
salt and black pepper, to taste
Red pepper flakes, to taste

Take a small pan n and add butter over medium heat.
Sauté the garlic in the butter, until fragrant.
Then add couscous to the pan and then cook for a minute.
Now, add the chicken broth and transfer to air fryer basket.
Air fry it for 25 minutes at 400 degrees F.
Serve warm and enjoy!

Calories 795 Total Fat 14.4g Saturated Fat 8.3g Cholesterol 33mg Sodium 704mg Total Carbohydrate 135.4g Dietary Fiber 8.7g Total Sugars 0.6g Protein 27.1g

Moroccan Vegetable Couscous

Prep: 12 Minutes | Cook Time: 35 Minutes | Makes: 2Servings

16-ounces chickpeas
4 bell peppers
1 onion
1 carrot
1 zucchini
1 cup kale
2 tablespoons mint
2 cups couscous
1tablespoon harissa
2 teaspoons garlic salt
4 teaspoons cumin powder
1 teaspoon turmeric powder
2 teaspoons paprika powder
1 tablespoons sumac

Clean and chop the veggies and keep them aside. Take a mixing bowl and add chickpeas, cumin, salt, and paprika powder to it. Toss the chickpeas in the bowl. cook in the air fryer for 15 minutes at 400 degrees F. Meanwhile, take a pan and sauté onion and zucchini by adding oil over medium heat. Then add harissa and cook for 5 minutes. In parallel, take another pan and cook the bell peppers in oil for 3 minutes. Preheat the air fryer to 400 degrees for a few minutes. Combine the kale with oil and salt and keep in the lined baking pan and cook for 20 minutes. Now, take a mixing bowl and add couscous with turmeric, cumin, and garlic salt. Then add the 2 cups of boiling water to the bowl and let it sit with the covering top. Once it is all set, add everything to the couscous and toss it in the bowl. Sprinkle mint leaves and sumac. Serve and enjoy!

Calories 1675 Total Fat 18g Saturated Fat 1.8g Cholesterol 3mg Sodium 225mg Total Carbohydrate 312.5g Dietary Fiber 56.2g Total Sugars 44.6g Protein 73.3g

Air-Fryer Chickpea Fritters with Sweet-Spicy Sauce

Prep: 12 Minutes | Cook Time:6 Minutes | Makes: 3Servings

1 cup yogurt
2 tablespoons sugar
1tablespoon honey
salt and black pepper, to taste
1/2 teaspoon red pepper flakes

FRITTERS:
3 cups chickpeas
1 teaspoon cumin
1/2 teaspoon salt
1/2 teaspoon garlic powder
1/2 teaspoon ginger
1 egg
1/2 teaspoon baking soda
1/2 cup cilantro
2 onions

Preheat the air fryer to 400°F. Take a mixing bowl and add the first six ingredients to the bowl. Then add the chickpeas to the food processor along with the seasonings. Now, add egg and baking soda to the food processor. Pulse it well. Transfer the mixture to the bowl and add cilantro, onions. Make balls from the chickpeas mixture and place them in the air fryer basket. Bake for 6 minutes and serve it with sauce. Enjoy!

Calories 895 Total Fat 14.9g Saturated Fat 2.6g Cholesterol 59mg Sodium 730mg Total Carbohydrate 148.9g Dietary Fibre 36.7g Total Sugars 44.3g Protein 46.3g

Air Fryer Falafel

Prep: 10 Minutes | Cook Time: 14 Minutes | Makes: 2 Servings

15 ounces chickpeas
2 cloves garlic
½ cup onion
½ cup parsley
½ cup cilantro
3 tablespoons wheat flour
1 teaspoon cumin
3/4 teaspoon kosher salt
1/2 teaspoon baking soda
1/2 teaspoon coriander
1/4 teaspoon black pepper
1/8 teaspoon cayenne powder

Add the chickpeas, garlic, onion, flour, baking soda, cilantro, parsley, cumin, cayenne, salt, coriander, and pepper to the bowl to the food processor. Pulse it coarsely and add little to it. Make balls from the mixture and place them in the air fryer. Cook at 350 degrees for 14 minutes. Once the balls get browned, serve and enjoy!

Calories 844 Total Fat 13.4g Saturated Fat 1.4g Cholesterol 0mg Sodium 1252mg Total Carbohydrate 143.4g Dietary Fibre 38.8g Total Sugars 24.2g Protein 43.5g

Air Fryer Healthy Zucchini Corn Fritters(GF)

Prep: 12 Minutes | Cook Time: 10 Minutes | Makes: 2Servings

2 zucchini
1 cup corn pearls
1 potato
2 tablespoons chickpea flour
2 crushed garlic
oil spray, for greasing
salt and pepper, to taste

For Serving:
Ketchup

Using a grater, grate the zucchini. Take a mixing bowl and add the grated zucchini with oil, pepper, and salt. Leave it out for 15 minutes and remove the excess water from the zucchini. Using a masher, mash the cooked potato. Take a mixing bowl and add zucchini, garlic, salt, potato, corn, chickpea flour, and pepper to it. Mix it well and make patties out of the mixture. Place the patties on the lined air fryer basket. Spray oil on the patties and cook for 5 minutes in the preheated air fryer. Turn the patties halfway through cooking and continue to cook for 5 minutes. Once it gets browned, serve the patties with ketchup. Enjoy!

Calories 195 Total Fat 1.5g Saturated Fat 0.2g Cholesterol 0mg Sodium 28mg Total Carbohydrate 37.5g Dietary Fiber 7.2g Total Sugars 7.4g Protein 7.5g

Lupini Beans Fritters(GF)

Prep: 20Minutes | Cook Time: 18 Minutes | Makes: 2 Servings

11-ounce lupini beans
1 cup zucchini
2 sliced spring onions
1-ounce hempseed

Seasoning
2 teaspoons paprika powder
1 teaspoon garlic powder
1 teaspoon chili powder
½ teaspoon onion powder
salt and black pepper, to taste

Drain and rinse the beans and peel the skin of them. In a food processor, add the beans, hem seeds, onions, zucchini, and seasoning and pulse it smooth. Make balls out of the mixture and roll into fritters. Arrange the fritters in the lined baking tray.
Set the temperature to 350 degrees F in the air fryer and cook for 18-22 minutes. Flip the fritters halfway through cooking. Serve and enjoy!

Calories 811 Total Fat 28.4g Saturated Fat 3g Cholesterol 0mg Sodium 4378mg Total Carbohydrate 77.1g Dietary Fiber 72.8g Total Sugars 2g Protein 67.5g

Black Bean Fritters(GF)

Prep: 12 Minutes | Cook Time: 12 Minutes | Makes: 2servings

Oil, as needed
15-ounce Black Beans
1/3 cup onion
1/4 cup cilantro
1 egg
2 teaspoons ginger
1 garlic clove
1 teaspoon cumin
1 teaspoon coriander
1 teaspoon salt
1/2 teaspoon hot pepper sauce
1/2 cup breadcrumbs

preheat the air fryer to 400 degrees F for a few minutes. Meanwhile, add all the ingredients to the food processor and pulse it smooth. Then form patties out of the mixture. Air fry the patties for 12 minutes, flipping halfway through. Once it becomes golden brown, remove and drain the patties in the paper towel. Repeat the same process for the remaining patties mixture. Serve warm and enjoy!

Calories 884 Total Fat 7g Saturated Fat 1.8g Cholesterol 82mg Sodium 1406mg Total Carbohydrate 156.3g Dietary Fiber 34.4g Total Sugars 7.3g Protein 53g

Chickpea Squash Fritters (GF)

Prep: 22 Minutes | Cook Time: 12 Minutes | Makes: 4 Servings

4 cups Butternut Squash
1 cup Onions
2 cups Chickpea flour
½ tablespoon crushed Garlic
1 teaspoon Lemon juice
3 tablespoons Parsley
Oil spray, for greasing

Spices:
1 teaspoon Cumin powder
1/2 teaspoon Turmeric powder
1/6 teaspoon Red Chili powder
1/6 teaspoon Salt

Take a mixing bowl and add shredded butternut squash, lemon juice, onions, chickpea flour, garlic, all the spices, and parsley to it. Then mix with clean hands and make balls out of the mixture. Make fritters from the balls and add them to the air fryer basket grease with oil. Cook for 12 minutes, flipping halfway through. When it gets browned, remove the fritters and drain using paper towels. Add parsley to the patties and serve with your favorite dip. Enjoy!

Calories 446 Total Fat 6.6g Saturated Fat 0.7g Cholesterol 0mg Sodium 132mg Total Carbohydrate 80.7g Dietary Fiber 21.1g Total Sugars 15.1g Protein 21.3g

Air Fryer Fried Rice with Sesame-Sriracha Sauce

Prep: 12 Minutes | Cook Time: 15 Minutes | Makes: 2Servings

2 cups cooked rice
1 tablespoon vegetable oil
2 teaspoons sesame oil
Salt and black pepper, to taste
1 teaspoon Sriracha
1 teaspoon soy sauce
1/2 teaspoon sesame seeds
2 eggs
1 cup frozen peas
1 cup carrots

Place the cooked rice, oil, and 1 tablespoon water in the bowl. Season the rice with salt and pepper in the bowl. Now, put the rice in the foiled cake pan and cook at 350°F for 8 minutes in an air fryer. Meanwhile, take a bowl and add Sriracha, sesame oil, soy sauce, and sesame seeds to it. Then add the beaten eggs to the rice and cook for 4 minutes in air fryer Once the egg is cooked, add the peas and carrots to the rice. Cook for 2 minutes and then serve the rice with sauce. Enjoy!

Calories 932 Total Fat 17.5g Saturated Fat 3.8g Cholesterol 164mg Sodium 333mg Total Carbohydrate 166g Dietary Fibre 8.3g Total Sugars 7g Protein 23.6g

Air Fryer Egg Fried Rice

Prep: 12 Minutes | Cook Time: 12 Minutes | Makes: 2servings

1/2 cup leftover rice, cooked
1/2 peas
1/4 cup stir fry mix
1 tablespoon extra virgin olive oil
2 tablespoon soy sauce
1 tablespoon Worcestershire sauce
2 tablespoon five-spice powder
2 eggs
1 teaspoon butter
salt & pepper

Pour the eggs in the ramekin and add butter, pepper, salt. Place the mixture in the air fryer and cook for 8 minutes at 360 degrees F. Once the egg is cooked, add the other ingredients to the bowl and mix it well. Now, combine everything with the rice. Then grease the skillet with oil and spread the rice in it. Cook the rice for 5 minutes. Once cooked, serve warm and enjoy!

Calories 274 Total Fat 13.6g Saturated Fat 3.6g Cholesterol 169mg Sodium 1137mg Total Carbohydrate 20.5g Dietary Fiber 8g Total Sugars 3.6g Protein 12.4g

Buffalo Quinoa Fritters(GF)

Prep: 12 Minutes | Cook Time: 25 Minutes | Makes: 2 Servings

1/2 cup Quinoa
1 cup water
1 cup cooked Chickpeas
1/4 cup Hot Sauce
1/2 cup Cheddar cheese
1 Egg
1/2 cup Panko
Salt and Pepper
2Oil
oil spray, for greasing

Take a saucepan and add water and quinoa to the pan. Cook the quinoa for 5 minutes. Once it is cooked well, allow the grains to cool. Meanwhile, cook the chickpeas in a saucepan. Once cooked, mash the chickpeas using a masher. Then add quinoa, egg, breadcrumbs, salt, chickpeas, hot sauce, Cheddar cheese, and pepper to the mixing bowl. Now, make patties out of the mixture. Mist the patties with oil. Air fry the patties at 177°C 350°F for 5 minutes. Once they are crispy, serve the patties and enjoy!

Calories 89 Total Fat 35.3g Saturated Fat 9.7g Cholesterol 112mg Sodium 1195mg Total Carbohydrate 108.4g Dietary Fibre 21.7g Total Sugars 13.1g Protein 38.9g

Lentil Fritters with Garlic Sauce

Prep: 15 Minutes | Cook Time: 20Minutes | Makes: 4Servings

2 cups cooked lentils
1 tablespoon olive oil
1onion
4 garlic cloves
8-ounces sliced mushrooms
1 cup cooked quinoa
1cup walnuts
1 teaspoon cumin
1 teaspoon smoked paprika
1 teaspoon dry parsley
¾ teaspoon salt
1 tablespoon flax powder
3 tablespoons water
2 teaspoons soy sauce

Garlic sauce
1 cup soy milk
2 tablespoons nutritional yeast
2 minced garlic
1tablespoon corn starch
salt, to taste

Cook the lentils in a pan for 10 minutes. Once it gets cooked well, keep them aside. Meanwhile, sauté the garlic, onion, and mushrooms in the pan for 5 minutes over medium heat. Pulse the walnuts to the fine powder and add it to the bowl. Add salt, egg, flax powder, spices, and mushroom mixture to the processor. Now, add the cooked lentils to the processor and make dough out of the mixture. Meanwhile, you can prepare the garlic sauce by mixing all the ingredients (mentioned under ingredients) in the hot pan for 5 minutes. Cook until the sauce gets thickened. Make patties out of the mixture and mist with oil spray, Add it to the air fryer basket and the air fryer for 10 minutes at 400 degrees F. Once the patties get browned, serve it with garlic sauce.

Calories 808 Total Fat 27.3g Saturated Fat 2.2g Cholesterol 0mg Sodium 487mg Total Carbohydrate 102g Dietary Fiber 37.5g Total Sugars 7g Protein 45.1g

Lentil Balls With Zesty Rice

Prep: 25Minutes | Cook Time: 30Minutes | Makes: 2 Servings

For the lentil balls:
2 cans lentils
1 cup walnut halves
3tablespoons dried mushrooms
2 tablespoons tomato paste
3tablespoons parsley
salt and black pepper, to taste
1 cup bread crumbs

For the zesty rice:
3 cups water
2 cups basmati rice
2 tablespoons lemon juice
2 tablespoons parsley
2 teaspoons lemon zest
1/6 teaspoon salt

To Garnish:
2 cups lettuce
1 cup cherry tomatoes
1 cup red onion
4 lemon wedges

Preheat the air fryer to 365 degrees F. In a food processor, add walnuts, dried mushrooms, lentils, tomato paste, parsley, salt, and pepper. Pulse it to smooth and then add the breadcrumbs to the lentil mixture. Make balls from the mixture and place them in the greased air fryer basket and cook for 10 minutes. Meanwhile, take a pot and add water and rice over medium heat. Cook for 20 minutes then add the lemon zest, parsley, lemon juice, and salt to it. Now, mix the lettuce, onions, and tomatoes and equally divide them between the plates. Then serve with lentil balls; garnish with lemon wedges.
Enjoy!

Calories 932 Total Fat 17.5g Saturated Fat 3.8g Cholesterol 164mg Sodium 333mg Total Carbohydrate 166g Dietary Fibre 8.3g Total Sugars 7g Protein 23.6g

Air Fryer Lentil Tacos

Prep: 5 Minutes | Cook Time: 6 Minutes | Makes: 2 Servings

10 hard taco shells
2 teaspoons of taco seasoning
2 cups lentils
2 teaspoons of fajita
1/4 cup grated parmesan cheese
Half bunch iceberg lettuce
1 chopped tomato
2 tablespoons sour cream
1 tablespoon chives

Preheat your air fryer to 350 degrees F. Take a mixing bowl and add the lentils and toss it with taco seasoning. Now, place the taco shells in the air fryer basket and add the lentils mixture to it. Top the taco shells with grated cheese. Bake the taco shells at 400 degrees C for 6 minutes. Once the cheese starts melting, top the taco shells with lettuce, chives, tomatoes, and sour cream. Enjoy!

Calories 1419 Total Fat 80.5g Saturated Fat 6.4g Cholesterol 228mg Sodium 5756mg Total Carbohydrate 106.1g Dietary Fiber 13.1g Total Sugars 11.3g Protein 81.9g

Air Fryer BBQ Lentil Meatballs

Prep: 20 Minutes | Cook Time: 35-40 Minutes | Makes: 4 Servings

2 cups vegetable broth
1 cup lentils
1/2 cup dried mushrooms
2 tablespoon avocado oil
1 cup onion
1 tablespoon tomato paste
1 garlic clove
1/2 cup wheat
3 tablespoon BBQ sauce
2 tablespoon vegetable broth
1 tablespoon soy sauce
1 teaspoon onion powder
1 teaspoon dried parsley
1/2 teaspoon smoked paprika
1/2 teaspoon salt
1/4 teaspoon black pepper

Take a pot and add vegetable broth, chopped mushrooms, and lentils, and cook over medium heat for 20 minutes. Meanwhile, take a saucepan and add oil over medium heat. Sauté onion in the pan for 5 minutes and then add the tomato paste, garlic cloves to the pan. Cook for a minute more. Then add the mushroom, onion mixture, parsley, smoked paprika, Worcestershire sauce, onion powder, wheat, 3tablespoonBBQ sauce, water to the food processor. Pulse it to smooth paste until the hummus is ready.

Now, make balls out of the mixture and place the balls in the greased air fryer. Drizzle oil over the lentil balls and cook at 350 degrees F for 12 minutes. Once the balls get browned, serve it to a plate with BBQ sauce. Enjoy!

Calories 412 Total Fat 2.8g 4% Saturated Fat 0.5g Cholesterol 0mg Sodium 1762mg Total Carbohydrate 78.7g Dietary Fiber 19.4g Total Sugars 23g Protein 19.3g

Air Fryer Fish Recipe Pecan Crusted Halibut(GF)

Prep: 15 Minutes | Cook Time: 8 Minutes | Makes: 4 Servings

2 pounds Halibut filets
1 cup pecan
1 cup Panko breadcrumbs
2 tablespoons lemon pepper
4 eggs
1 cup cornstarch
1 cup white wine
Lemon wedges

Remove the skin of the halibut fillets and keep them aside. Take a bowl and whisk the egg along with cornstarch. Then add white wine to the flour and mix it well. Now, add lemon pepper to the mixture and prepare it like a thick batter. Pulse the pecans to a fine powder using a food processor. Mix the pecans and breadcrumbs. Then coat the halibut in the egg wash and then in the bread crumb mixture. Preheat the air fryer to 350 degrees F. Place the fillets in the air fryer and cook for 8 minutes. Once the fish gets cooked, serve the fish with lemon wedges.

Calories 54 Total Fat 9.9g Saturated Fat 2.4g Cholesterol 204mg Sodium 179mg Total Carbohydrate 38g Dietary Fibre 1.7g Total Sugars 1g Protein 47.3g

Air Fryer Fish Sticks (Halibut-Cod)

Prep: 12 Minutes | Cook Time: 8 Minutes | Makes: 2 Servings

1 pound of filets cod/halibut
2 cups corn flakes
1/4 cup wheat flour
1 egg
1/2 cup milk
salt and pepper, to taste
½ cup mayonnaise
Sriracha sauce, as needed

Clean and cut the fillets into sticks. Take a mixing bowl and add cornflakes, flour, salt, and pepper and mix it well. In another bowl, add the egg and milk; whisk it together. Coat the fish sticks in the egg mixture and rub in the cornflakes mixture. Arrange the fish sticks in the air fryer basket and cook at 350 degrees F for 8 minutes. Flip the sticks halfway through cooking. Once it is cooked well, add Sriracha to the mayo and serve with sticks. Enjoy!

Calories 507 Total Fat 23.7g Saturated Fat 4.3g Cholesterol 102mg Sodium 782mg Total Carbohydrate 53.5g Dietary Fiber 1.7g Total Sugars 8.5g Protein 21.3g

The Easiest Air Fryer Salmon(GF)

Prep: 10 Minutes | Cook Time: 8 Minutes | Makes: 1-2 Servings

10 ounces Salmon
2 tablespoon orange juice
3 tablespoon soy sauce
1 garlic clove
1 tablespoon sriracha
Sesame seeds
Scallions

Take a mixing bowl and add orange juice, Sriracha, garlic, and soy sauce and whisk it well. Then marinate the fish in the mixture and allow the marinade for 20 minutes. Now, place the fish in the air fryer basket and cook for 8 minutes at 390 degrees F. Once the fish is cooked well, sprinkle sesame seeds and diced scallions. Serve and enjoy!

Calories 490 Total Fat 22.1g Saturated Fat 3.1g Cholesterol 125mg Sodium 2940mg Total Carbohydrate 14.1g Dietary Fibre 2g Total Sugars 3.8g Protein 60.3g

Air Fryer Tilapia With Garlic & Lemon (GF)

Prep: 20 Minutes | Cook Time: 12 Minutes | Makes: 3 Servings

18-ounces tilapia filets
2 tablespoons of olive oil
1/2 teaspoon garlic powder
1/2 teaspoon lemon pepper seasoning
salt and black pepper, to taste
Chopped parsley
Lemon wedges

Pre-heat air fryer to 350°F for 5 minutes. Take a mixing bowl and add oil, lemon pepper, garlic powder, salt, and pepper to it. Then add the fillets to the bowl and coat it well. Line the air fryer basket with parchment paper or grease it using oil and place the fish fillets. Cook the fish at 350°F for 12 minutes. Once the fish is cooked well, sprinkle with parsley leaves and serve with lemon wedges. Adjust the seasoning as per your preference. Enjoy!

Calories 310 Total Fat 14.5g Saturated Fat 3.4g Cholesterol 100mg Sodium 672mg Total Carbohydrate 2.1g Dietary Fibre 0.9g 3% Total Sugars 0.3g Protein 44.7g

Lemon Caper Cod

Prep: 12 Minutes | Cook Time: 8 Minutes | Makes: 2 Servings

2 cod fillets
Sea salt and pepper, to taste
2 tablespoons lemon juice
2 tablespoons of olive oil
1tablespoon caper
½ teaspoon lemon zest

Add salt and pepper to the cod fillets and place them on the greased basket of the air fryer. Then drizzle one teaspoon of oil over the fish and bake at 360°F for 4 minutes. Meanwhile, combine the remaining oil with capers, lemon zest, and juice. Spread the mixture over the fish and continue cooking for 4 minutes. Once the fish becomes flakes, serve and enjoy!

Calories 215 Total Fat 15.2g Saturated Fat 2.1g Cholesterol 55mg Sodium 201mg Total Carbohydrate 0.6g Dietary Fibre 0.2g Total Sugars 0.4g Protein 20.2g

Air Fryer Fried Calamari

Prep: 20 Minutes | Cook Time: 8 Minutes | Makes: 2 Servings

16 ounces calamari rings
1 cup buttermilk
2 cups whole wheat flour
½ cup cornstarch
1 teaspoon dried oregano
½ teaspoon salt
½ teaspoon black pepper
1 teaspoon sweet paprika
¼ teaspoon cayenne
Cooking oil spray
few Lemon wedges
½ cup of Marinara sauce

Take a mixing bowl and add buttermilk to the calamari rings and refrigerate for 1 hour. Preheat the air fryer to 400 degrees F. Meanwhile, take a mixing bowl and add flour, salt, pepper, paprika, cornstarch, oregano, and cayenne to it. Mix it well. Then coat the rings in the flour mixture and place it on the air fryer; drizzle cooking oil spray over the fish. Cook for 4 minutes and flip them through halfway cooking. Continue to cook for another 4 minutes. Serve the fish with marinara sauce and lemon wedges. Enjoy!

Calories 1179 Total Fat 28.9g Saturated Fat 1.4g Cholesterol 120mg Sodium 1872mg Total Carbohydrate 186.5g Dietary Fibre 11.9g Total Sugars 11.9g Protein 40.1g

Cod Fillet in Parchment

Prep: 10 Minutes | Cook Time: 15 Minutes | Makes: 2 Servings

1 pounds cod fillets
2 cups grape tomatoes
¼ cup sliced olives
1 lemon zest
2 tablespoons lemon juice
2 crushed garlic cloves
1 tablespoon extra virgin olive oil
salt and pepper, to taste

Preheat the air fryer to 350 degrees F. Line the air fryer basket with your parchment paper. Take a mixing bowl and add the tomatoes, garlic, lemon zest, salt, olives, lemon juice, and pepper to it. Clean and pat dry the fish and add oil, salt, and pepper to it. Then place the fish and veggies in the lining paper and seal it tightly. Bake the fish for 15 minutes in the air fryer. Once cooked, sprinkle with lemon juice and serve. Enjoy!

Calories 311 Total Fat 11.4g Saturated Fat 1.4g Cholesterol 111mg Sodium 301mg Total Carbohydrate 12.1g Dietary Fibre 3.6g Total Sugars 5.8g Protein 42.7g

Air Fryer Greek Salmon

Prep: 12 Minutes | Cook Time: 8 Minutes | Makes: 2 Servings

For the Salmon:
1 pound salmon fillets
1 tablespoon olive oil
1 lemon juice
2 garlic cloves
½ teaspoon dried oregano
½ teaspoon dried dill
¼ teaspoon red pepper flakes
Required Salt and pepper

For the Greek Salad:
4 tablespoons extra virgin olive oil
2tablespoons red wine vinegar
½ teaspoon dried oregano
3 tomatoes
½ English cucumbers
½ small red onions
4 ounces sliced black kalamata olives
Parsley
salt and black pepper, to taste
1ounce Feta Cheese

Take a mixing bowl and add oil, lemon juice, dill, garlic, oregano, and red pepper flakes to it. Then add fillets to the bowl and toss it well. Marinate the fish in the mixture for 15 minutes, Grease the air fryer basket with oil or spray. Place the fillets in the air fryer basket and cook at 400°F for 9 minutes. Meanwhile, combine all the Greek salad ingredients in a bowl. Once the fish becomes flaky, serve it along with the salad and enjoy!

Calories 1439 Total Fat 106.7g Saturated Fat 19g Cholesterol 225mg Sodium 615mg Total Carbohydrate 32.6g Dietary Fibre 8.8g Total Sugars 16.9g Protein 99.4g

Crispy Air Fryer Tilapia

Prep: 8 Minutes | Cook Time: 10 Minutes | Makes: 3 Servings

6 Tilapia Fish Fillet
3 Cups Bread Crumbs
1 Egg
1 Teaspoon warm water
Olive Oil Spray

Seasoning:
2 tablespoons Lemon Pepper Seasoning
2 tablespoons Paprika Powder
1 Teaspoon Garlic Powder
salt, to taste

Take a mixing bowl and crack the egg and water, whisk it well. In another bowl, add the seasoning ingredients and breadcrumbs together. Line the air fryer basket with foil paper. Now, coat the fillet in the egg mixture, then in the breadcrumbs. Arrange the fillets in the air fryer basket and drizzle oil over it. Cook the fish at 350°F for 10 minutes. Flip the fish halfway to cooking and continue to cook. Once the fish is browned, serve the fish with salad. Enjoy!

Calories 963 Total Fat 31.5g Saturated Fat 5.8g Cholesterol 105mg Sodium 1824mg Total Carbohydrate 127.3g Dietary Fibre 8.1g Total Sugars 9.1g Protein 40.9g

Air Fryer Fish Tacos (GF)

Prep: 16 Minutes | Cook Time: 8 Minutes | Makes: 2 Servings

For the Fish Coating:
1/4 cup mayo
1 tablespoon lemon juice
1/2 teaspoon garlic powder
1/2 teaspoon black pepper
1/4 teaspoon salt
1 teaspoon chili powder
1 teaspoon oregano

For the Panko Coating Mixture.
2 cups Panko bread crumbs
1 teaspoon chili powder
1/2 teaspoon salt
1/2 teaspoon oregano
1/4 teaspoon black pepper

For Frying:
2 tablespoon oil

Preheat the air fryer at 400 degrees F for 5 minutes. Clean and cut the fillets into pieces and coat them in the mayo mixture. Take a mixing bowl and add the Panko breadcrumbs coatings and mix it well. In another bowl, mix all the spices. Add the fish to the spice mixture and coat the fish in the breadcrumbs mixture. Make sure the fillets get coated enough and place the fish in the air fryer basket. Cook the fillets for 8 minutes and flip the fillets halfway through cooking. Once the fish becomes flaky, serve and enjoy!
You can also follow some additional steps for Fish Tacos. In the tortillas, add the chipotle sauce, cilantro, chopped avocados, lime juice tomatoes, and place the fish and top with salsa sauce.
Serve and enjoy!

Calories 1467 Total Fat 89.3g Saturated Fat 16.3g Cholesterol 8mg Sodium 1838mg 80 Total Carbohydrate 151.3g Dietary Fibre 26.5g Total Sugars 13.7g Protein 28.2g

To make Air Fryer Fish Tacos:
7 tortillas
1/2 cup chipotle ranch sauce
1/4 cup cilantro
2 chopped avocados
1 chopped tomato
4 diced scallions
Lime juice
1/4 cup salsa

Air Fryer White Fish With Garlic & Lemon(GF)

Prep: 12 Minutes | Cook Time: 8 Minutes | Makes: 2 Servings

10 ounces tilapia filets
2 teaspoons of olive oil
1/2 teaspoon garlic powder
1/2 teaspoon lemon pepper seasoning
Salt and black pepper, to taste
Topping:

Chopped parsley
Lemon wedges

Pre-heat Air Fryer to 400 degrees F for 5 minutes. Clean and dry the fillets; brush oil over the fillets and season with lemon pepper, salt, garlic powder, and pepper. Place the seasoned fish on the greased air fryer basket. Cook the fish at 400 degrees F, for 8 minutes. Once the fish gets browned, sprinkle parsley and serve the fish with lemon wedges. Enjoy!

Calories 239 Total Fat 9.1g Saturated Fat 2.4g Cholesterol 83mg Sodium 567mg Total Carbohydrate 3.1g Dietary Fiber 1.3g Total Sugars 0.5g Protein 37.8g

Air Fryer Pesto Salmon Recipe(GF)

Prep: 15 Minutes | Cook Time:13 Minutes | Makes: 2 Servings

For the Salmon:
4 salmon filets
1 tablespoon avocado oil
Salt & pepper
1/2 cup parmesan cheese

For the Pesto:
2 cups basil
1/4 cup pecans
1 teaspoon salt
1/4 teaspoon pepper
Garlic cloves
1 teaspoon lemon zest
1cup olive oil

Add all pesto ingredients to the food processor. Pulse it to form a smooth paste. Transfer the mixture to the bowl and the cheese to the mixture. Preheat the air fryer to 400°F for 3 minutes. Clean and pat dry the salmon with a paper towel. Then season the salmon with oil, salt, and pepper. Arrange the salmon in the air fryer basket and cook for 10 minutes. Once the fish becomes flaky, top it with pesto. Serve and enjoy!

Calories 1772 Total Fat 111.7g Saturated Fat 15.6g Cholesterol 5mg Sodium 2803mg Total Carbohydrate 40.1g Dietary Fibre 0.8g Total Sugars 0.2g Protein 3.3g

Blackened Salmon With Creamy Lemon Caper Sauce (GF)

Prep: 20 Minutes | Cook Time: 8 Minutes | Makes: 2 Servings

4 Salmon filets
Olive Oil Spray

Seasoning Ingredients:
1 tablespoon Paprika
1/2 teaspoon thyme
½ teaspoon Oregano
1 teaspoon Onion Powder
1/2 teaspoon Garlic Powder
salt and black pepper, to taste
1/2 teaspoon Chili Powder
1/8 teaspoon Cayenne

For Creamy Lemon Caper Sauce:

1/2 cup Plain Greek Yogurt
1 Lemon zest & juice
1 teaspoon garlic minced
2 teaspoons capers
1tablespoonFresh Parsley
Salt & Pepper to taste

Mix all Creamy Lemon Caper Sauce ingredients in a bowl and set aside for later. Take a mixing bowl and combine the seasoning in the bowl. Grease the air fryer basket with olive oil spray. Arrange the salmon in the air fryer basket and add the seasoning mixture over the fish. Spray oil over the top of the fish and cook at 370°F for 10 minutes. Once the fish becomes flaky, serve the fish with yogurt sauce and lemon caper sauce. Serve and enjoy!

Calories 890 Total Fat 9g Saturated Fat 0.2g Cholesterol 0mg Sodium 1668mg Total Carbohydrate 42.8g Dietary Fibre 2g Total Sugars 1.1g   Protein 1.1g

Pistachio Crusted Fish

Prep: 20 Minutes | Cook Time: 10 Minutes | Makes: 2 Servings

**¼ cup crumbled feta
2 tablespoons chopped pistachio
2 tablespoons Panko breadcrumbs
1 chopped scallion
½ teaspoon lemon zest
2 halibut fillets
1 teaspoon olive oil
1/6 teaspoon garlic powder
salt, to taste
few Lemon wedges, optional**

Preheat the air fryer to 400 degrees F for 5 minutes. Take a mixing bowl and add the feta, breadcrumbs, scallion, pistachios, and lemon zest to it. Clean and pat dry the fish fillets and season them with oil, garlic powder, and salt. Cook the fish for 10 minutes at 350 degrees F in the air fryer. Once the fish becomes flaky and tender, serve it with the topping of cheese and breadcrumbs.

Calories 801 Total Fat 22.3g Saturated Fat 7.2g Cholesterol 110mg Sodium 464mg Total Carbohydrate 19g Dietary Fiber 1g Total Sugars 1.5g   Protein 67g

Creamy Fish Chowder(GF)

Prep: 20 Minutes | Cook Time:15 Minutes | Makes: 2 Servings

**2 tablespoons butter
1 onion chopped
1/2 cup white wine
2 cups clam juice
2 Yukon gold potatoes
2 celery stalks
2 pounds skinless codfish , fillets
1tablespoon thyme leaves
1 teaspoon Old Bay seasoning
salt and black pepper, to taste
2 cups half-and-half
½ teaspoon fish sauce**

Take a pan and melt the unsalted butter over medium heat. Then add the celery, chopped onion, salt, and pepper and cook for 7 minutes. Now, add the potatoes, thyme, clam juice, white wine, and old bay seasoning to the pan. Continue to cook for 15 minutes with the lid on top at a low flame. Meanwhile, add a fish fillet to the air fryer and cook for 6 minutes, flipping halfway through, at 360°F. Now add cooked fillets to a pan along with milk and cream. Stir and cook for 4-5 minutes, then add fish sauce and stir twice. Serve the fish sprinkled with chopped chives and enjoy!

Calories 744 Total Fat 40.3g Saturated Fat 24.7g Cholesterol 120mg Sodium 1728mg Total Carbohydrate 94.5g Dietary Fibre 6.3g Total Sugars 13.7g   Protein 13.2g

Air Fryer Swai Fish (GF)

Prep: 10 Minutes | Cook Time: Minutes | Makes: 2 Servings

18 ounces Swai filets
1 teaspoon olive oil
¼ teaspoon of Blackened seasoning
oil spray, for greasing

Preheat the air fryer to 400°F. Grease the air fryer basket with oil spray and line with parchment paper. Season the Swai fillets with oil and blackened seasoning and toss it well. Place the fish in the air fryer basket and cook for minutes. Flip the fish halfway cooking and continue to cook for 3 minutes. Serve the fish with salad and enjoy!

Calories 587 Total Fat 38.7g Saturated Fat 18.4g Cholesterol 56mg Sodium 1197mg Total Carbohydrate 22.6g Dietary Fibre 0g Total Sugars 6.8g Protein 33.9g

Air Fryer Catfish

Prep: 15 Minutes | Cook Time: 8 Minutes | Makes: 3 Servings

6 catfish fillets
1/2 cup cornmeal, crushed
1/6 teaspoon salt
2 tablespoons of Olive oil

Preheat Air Fryer at 400degrees F for a few minutes. Clean and pat dry the catfish. Add the fillets, salt, olive oil, and cornmeal to the zip-lock bag and shake gently. Then cook the fish in the air fryer for 8 minutes at 400 degrees F. Once the fish becomes flaky, serve and enjoy!

Calories 586 Total Fat 34.4g Saturated Fat 5.9g Cholesterol 150mg Sodium 305mg Total Carbohydrate 15.6g Dietary Fibre 1.5g Total Sugars 0.1g   Protein 51.4g

Tuna Steaks Recipe

Prep: 10 Minutes | Cook Time: 8 Minutes | Makes: 2 Servings

For Tuna Steaks
2 large Mahi tuna steaks
1 teaspoon olive oil
salt and pepper, to taste

For The Dipping Sauce

2 Green onions
2 tablespoon soy sauce
1 tablespoon lime juice
1 tablespoon water
1/2 teaspoon crushed garlic

Preheat the air fryer at 400 degrees F for 5 minutes. Season the Mahi tuna steaks with salt, olive oil, and pepper. Place the steaks in the air fryer basket and cook at 400 degrees F for 4 minutes. Flip the tuna steaks halfway through cooking. In a mixing bowl, add the coconut amino, water, green onion, lime juice, and garlic to it. Once the fish becomes flaky, serve the fish with dip sauce. Enjoy!

Calories 239 Total Fat 5.7g Saturated Fat 1.2g Cholesterol 73mg Sodium 1256mg Total Carbohydrate 4.4g Dietary Fibre 0.6g Total Sugars 1g   Protein 41.5g

Pepper Chili Prawns

Prep: 10 Minutes | Cook Time: 3 Minutes | Makes: 2 Servings

1 cup Shrimp
2 eggs
¼ teaspoon chopped Green chilies
¼ teaspoon chopped Garlic.
1/2 teaspoon Pepper powder
1/2 teaspoon red chili paste
1 teaspoon Cornstarch
1 teaspoon flour
1/2 teaspoon Soia sauce
1/2 teaspoon Green chili sauce
1 teaspoon sugar
1 teaspoon Vinegar
Oil
1 cup Bread crumbs

Preheat the air fryer at 400 degrees F for 3 minutes Take a large mixing bowl and add all the ingredients except bread crumbs to it. Then coat the shrimps in the bread crumb mixture well; drizzle oil over the shrimps. Cook the shrimp for 3 minutes and shake while halfway cooking. Once it is cooked, serve and enjoy!

Calories 373 Total Fat 14.5g Saturated Fat 3g Cholesterol 187mg Sodium 606mg Total Carbohydrate 44.4g Dietary Fiber 2.5g Total Sugars 6.1g Protein 15.6g

Greek Salad with Air Fryer Salmon

Prep: 20 Minutes | Cook Time:8 Minutes | Makes: 2 Servings

10-ounces Salmon filet
1 tablespoon extra virgin olive oil
1 tablespoon dried basil
1 tablespoon dried oregano

Fr the Greek Salad:
1 diced cucumber
1/2 cup cherry tomatoes
1/4 cup diced onion
1/4 cup feta cheese
2 tablespoons kalamata olives
1/4 cup vinaigrette

Remaining Ingredients:
2 cups butter lettuce
1 avocado
1 lemon
1tablespoon dill

In a bowl, marinate the salmon with oil, basil, and oregano for 10 minutes. Then place the salmon in the air fryer and cook at 390°F for 8 minutes. Meanwhile, combine the diced red onion, olives, cucumber, halved cherry tomatoes, and feta cheese in the bowl. Now, add the vinaigrette to the mixture. On a platter, place the lettuce leaves, add the Greek salad, avocados, and cooked salmon. Then add more feta cheese as a topping to the salad and sprinkle lemon juice and dill. Serve the fish with vinaigrette and enjoy!

Calories 2688 Total Fat 67.9g Saturated Fat 11g Cholesterol 17mg Sodium 4237mg Total Carbohydrate 121g Dietary Fibre 11g Total Sugars 7.7g Protein 7.4g

Greek Air Fryer Chicken Kabobs (GF)

Prep: 15 Minutes | Cook Time: 15 Minutes | Makes: 2 Servings

For Marinade:
½ cup red wine vinegar
1/3 cup olive oil
2 tablespoons dried oregano
3 cloves garlic
2 tablespoon parsley (chopped finely)
½ teaspoon salt
½ teaspoon pepper

For Chicken Kabobs:
2 pounds chicken breasts (chopped)
2 sweet bell peppers (chopped)
1 onion (chopped)
8 ounces white button mushrooms

Begin by mixing all the ingredients of the marinade and putting the chicken in the mixed marinade. Make sure to coat the chicken completely with the marinade, letting it rest in the refrigerator for about 6 to 8 hours. Once the chicken has rested in the marinade for a good amount of time, take the chicken and thread it through a skewer, interchanging between the chicken and vegetables.

Put the skewered chicken in the air fryer cooking everything for about 5 minutes at around 380 degrees. Once the skewers are done, put the kabobs on a serving plate and serve it with a drizzle of Greek marinade and some parsley.

Calories 635 Total Fat 34.2g Saturated Fat 7.1g Cholesterol 202mg Sodium 495mg Total Carbohydrate 11.7g Dietary Fiber 3.1g Total Sugars 5.4g Protein 68.8

Greek Baked Chicken Wings

Prep: 15 Minutes | Cook Time: 25 Minutes | Makes: 4Servings

For Marinade
½ cup extra virgin olive oil
2 lemons (zest, juiced)
6 cloves garlic (peeled, crushed)
1 ½ tablespoons dried oregano
1 tablespoon black pepper
Salt , to taste
1 teaspoon sweet pepper
1 teaspoon cayenne pepper (optional)

For wings:

3 pounds chicken wings
Feta cheese (crumbled)
Sliced lemon (for garnish)

Try making the marinade for the chicken a few hours before preparation. To make the marinade, whisk together the lemon juice and extra virgin olive oil together before adding in all the other ingredients. Add the cayenne pepper only if you want to make the wings spicy. Add in the chicken wings once all the ingredients are mixed, and coat the wings throughout making sure to cover all the wings properly. Let the coated chicken wings rest in the fridge for a few hours or overnight. Preheat the air fryer to 400 degrees F. Shift the chicken to a basket lined with some parchment paper and let the wings bake for about 25 minutes in the preheated oven. Once the internal temperature of the wings becomes 165 degrees (can be checked using a thermometer) they will be cooked, once they reach that temperature take them out and let them boil for 5 minutes so it gets a nice golden brown and crispy skin. Once done, serve it on a serving plate and serve it with a side of lemon slices, and a garnish of feta cheese and parsley.

Calories 923 Total Fat 52.9g Saturated Fat 12g Cholesterol 311mg Sodium 441mg Total Carbohydrate 9.2g Dietary Fibre 2.6g Total Sugars 2.8g Protein 101.1g

Shake 'N Bake Style chicken

Prep: 10 Minutes | Cook Time: 25 Minutes | Makes: 4 Servings

2 pounds chicken thighs or drumsticks
Eggs or milk (too moisten the chicken)
1 cup Shake 'n bake' seasoned coating mix
Spraying oil

Begin by heating the oven to around 182°C (360°F). Start by coating the chicken with eggs or milk, depending on the ingredient used, making sure to coat the chicken all the way. Once the chicken is moist, add in the seasoned coating and coat the chicken with the mix, making sure to chicken is completely coated. Grease the air fryer basket with some oil, and coat the chicken with oil also. Put these coated chicken pieces on the air fryer basket on a single layer, making sure the chicken pieces are not touching each other, after about half the time turn over the chicken and let it cook some more. Cook the chicken pieces in the air fryer for about 25 minutes at 182°C (360°F), flipping them after some time. While cooking, spray the dry spots, continuing the frying until the internal temperature of the chicken reaches 75°C (165°F).

Calories 373 Total Fat 14.5g Saturated Fat 3g Cholesterol 187mg Sodium 606mg Total Carbohydrate 44.4g Dietary Fiber 2.5g Total Sugars 6.1g Protein 15.6g

Air Fryer Green Chili Chicken Bake

Prep: 14 Minutes | Cook Time: 20 Minutes | Makes: 2 Servings

Ingredients
4 flour tortillas
16 oz. chicken (shredded)
1 cup Green Chile Salsa
½ cup Sour Cream
8 oz. Monterey Jack and Habanero (shredded)

Start by putting the tortillas at the bottom of the air fryer so it covers its bottom.
Put ¼ of the chicken on one of the tortillas, take a bowl and mix some salsa and sour cream, pour ¼ of this over the chicken, and then ¼ of the cheese.
Cover the tortilla with the other tortillas and repeat the process, at the last tortilla top it off with the remaining cheese and salsa.
Let it cook in the air fryer for about 20 minutes at 190°C (375°F).
Once done, serve it with the garnish of cilantro, pico de Gallo, and guacamole if desired.

Calories 1010 Total Fat 52.3g Saturated Fat 29.7g Cholesterol 340mg Sodium 1235mg Total Carbohydrate 24.3g Dietary Fiber 3.1g Total Sugars 1.4g Protein 99.1g

Air fried Loaded Chicken with Potatoes(GF)

Prep: 12 Minutes | Cook Time: 20 Minutes | Makes: 2 Servings

1 pound chicken breasts
1 onion
2 tablespoon oil
1 teaspoon salt
1 teaspoon Garlic powder
½ teaspoon Black pepper
1 ½ cup Cheddar cheese (shredded)
3 green onions
2 potatoes

Begin by slicing the potatoes in half and chopping the onions into large chunks. Dice the chicken to about 1-inch chunks. Put both the diced chicken and potatoes in a zip lock bag, and add the onions, oil, salt, garlic powder, and black pepper to it. Seal the bag up and mix everything so the chicken and potatoes are coated throughout. Grease the basket of the air fryer with some oil and put the potatoes, chicken, and onions in it, cooking everything for about 20 minutes at 204°C (400°F), shaking the mix one or two times. When done, add some cheese, and bacon on top and broil everything for 5 minutes. Once done, serve it with a garnish of green onions.

Calories 928 Total Fat 58.6g 75% Saturated Fat 24.3g 121%
Cholesterol 291mg 97% Sodium 1890mg 82% Total Carbohydrate 9.2g 3%
Dietary Fibre 2.1g 7% Total Sugars 3.6g
Protein 88g

Creamy Air fried Chicken Broccoli Rice

Prep: 15 Minutes | Cook Time: 15 Minutes | Makes: 2 Servings

2 pounds chicken breasts
(boneless, skinless, sliced)
2 cups instant rice (white or brown)
3/4cup cream soup
2 cups Broccoli Florets
1 tablespoon garlic powder
1 tablespoon onion powder
3 tablespoon Parsley (dried)
½ teaspoon chili powder
3 cups broccoli (chopped)

Begin by heating the air fryer to around 390 degrees F. In a bowl, mix the spices and seasonings, coating it evenly on the chicken breasts. Take about 6 pieces of foil and put the rice, 1/6 part of the chicken, topping everything off with 2 tablespoons of cream soup and ½ cup broccoli. Add about ½ cup water in each foil packet and fold it tightly making sure the moisture cannot escape from the foil and cook it all for about 15 minutes. Once done, take everything out and serve on a serving plate.

Calories 854 Total Fat 19.5g Saturated Fat 5.7g Cholesterol 206mg
Sodium 977mg Total Carbohydrate 88.9g Dietary Fiber 3.3g
Total Sugars 2g Protein 75.5g

Chicken Stuffing Casserole

Prep: 25 Minutes | Cook Time: 45 Minutes | Makes: 2 Servings

1 ½ cup rotisserie chicken
(shredded)
2 tablespoons of olive oil
10 oz. bacon soup cream
(condensed)
1/3 cup whole milk
1 box stove top stuffing (cooked according to package instructions)

Begin by heating the air fryer to about 350 degrees F. Grease an oven-safe baking dish with some olive oil and put the chicken on the bottom of the pan. Take a bowl to mix the cream of bacon soup and milk, pouring it on top of the chicken once done. Cook the box stuffing and put it on top of the chicken. Once everything is layered, put it in the air fryer cooking everything for about 30 minutes, turning everything halfway.

Calories 201 Total Fat 10.5g Saturated Fat 3.5g Cholesterol 16mg
Sodium 759mg Total Carbohydrate 21g Dietary Fiber 2.7g
Total Sugars 4.6g Protein 5.4g

Garlicky Lemon Chicken Drumsticks(GF)

Prep: 15 Minutes | Cook Time: 20 Minutes | Makes: 4 Servings

8 Chicken Drumsticks
2 lemons
2 teaspoons Black pepper
1.5 teaspoon Smoked Paprika
1.5 teaspoon garlic powder
1 teaspoon onion powder
1 teaspoon oregano
1 tablespoon Lemon Zest (optional)

Take a bowl and add the chicken and lemon juice in it, coating the chicken thoroughly with the chicken. Once the chicken is moist, add all listed spices and rub it around the drumsticks, marinating everything for about 30 minutes or an hour.

Once they have been marinated for a long enough time, put them in the air fryer in a single layer and cook them for about 20 minutes at 400 degrees F.

Once done, take it out and serve it with a garnish of lemon zest and fried vegetables.

Calories 176 Total Fat 5.5g Saturated Fat 1.4g Cholesterol 81mg Sodium 76mg Total Carbohydrate 5.3g Dietary Fiber 1.7g Total Sugars 1.3g Protein 26.1g

Air Fried Chicken Shawarma

Prep: 15 Minutes | Cook Time: 15 Minutes | Makes: 2Servings

1 ½ pound chicken breasts (boneless)
4 Naan bread/pita bread, whole wheat

Spices :
2 tablespoons olive oil
2 cloves garlic (minced)
1 lemon's juice
1 teaspoon cumin (grounded)
1 teaspoon paprika
½ teaspoon allspice (grounded)
¼ teaspoon turmeric (grounded)
¼ teaspoon cinnamon (grounded)
1 teaspoon salt
½ teaspoon black pepper 9 grounded0

Tahini Sauce:
½ cup tahini sesame paste
½ lemon's juice
¼ cup water (warm)
¼ teaspoon cumin (grounded)
1 garlic clove (minced)
¼ teaspoon salt
2 teaspoon parsley

Start by making the marinade for the chicken, for which, add the olive oil, lemon juice, garlic, and other all listed spices in a bowl, giving a whisk until everything is well combined. Slice the chicken breasts lengthwise and put them in a ziplock bag. Add the marinade over the chicken inside the ziplock bag and massage the marinade all over the chicken. Let the chicken rest inside of the marinade for at least 6 hours inside a fridge, but if time is available, let it stay overnight. Then heat the oven to around 380 degrees F. Shift the chicken from the marinade to the air fryer and cook it for about 8 to 10 minutes, making sure to flip it halfway for even cooking throughout.

Tahini Sauce
For the tahini sauce, add water, lemon juice, tahini paste, garlic, cumin, and salt inside a food processor and pulse the mix until all the ingredients are well combined and turn into a creamy texture. If the constancy is not as desired, more water can be added.

Tomato Cucumber Salad
To make the salad mix all listed ingredients in a dish and toss everything to combine all the ingredients, once done season the tomato salad with some salt and pepper. For assembly of Shawarma, drizzle some oil on both sides of the Naan and put it in the air fryer at 400 degrees for around 2 minutes on each side, or till the crust becomes nice and crispy. Spread some homemade tahini sauce on top and add the salad, finish it off by adding the chicken made earlier, roll it to close all ends, and drizzle some more tahini sauce. The chicken Shawarma can also be wrapped with a siren wrap or foil to hold everything together.

Tomato Cucumber Salad:

1 cup tomatoes (diced)
1 English cucumber
2 tablespoons onion (minced)
½ lemon's juice
1 teaspoon red wine
2 teaspoon olive oil
2 tablespoon parsley
Salt and Pepper (to taste)

Calories 854 Total Fat 19.5g Saturated Fat 5.7g Cholesterol 206mg Sodium 977mg Total Carbohydrate 88.9g Dietary Fiber 3.3g Total Sugars 2g Protein 75.5g

Air Fried Lemon Pepper Drumsticks(GF)

Prep: 15 Minutes | Cook Time: 25 Minutes | Makes: 4Servings

8 chicken drumsticks
1 tablespoon lemon pepper seasoning
½ teaspoon garlic powder
2 teaspoon baking powder
½ teaspoon paprika
1 ½ tablespoon lemon juice
4 tablespoons olive oil

Begin by coating the drumsticks with a mixture of baking powder, paprika, and garlic powder. Put these coated drumsticks in the air fryer and air-fry the drumsticks for about 25 minutes at 375 degrees F. The chicken will be ready once the outside skin turns golden brown and the internal temperature of the chicken is at least165 degrees. Meanwhile, mix olive oil, lemon pepper seasoning, and some lemon juice inside a bowl and the drumsticks in them once they are done, make sure the drumsticks are coated on all sides.

Calories 267 Total Fat 16.9g Saturated Fat 8.8g Cholesterol 111mg Sodium 160mg Total Carbohydrate 2.7g Dietary Fiber 0.6g 2% Total Sugars 0.3g Protein 25.8g

Chicken legs(GF)

Prep: 15 Minutes | Cook Time: 20 Minutes | Makes: 2Servings

8 chicken drumsticks
2 tablespoon olive oil
Spices ingredients
1 teaspoon sea salt
½ teaspoon black pepper
1 teaspoon garlic powder
1 ½ teaspoon smoked paprika
¼ teaspoon chili powder
1 teaspoon onion powder

Begin by preheating the air fryer to around 400 degrees F. Take a bowl and mix in all the spices and herbs in it. Put the chicken drumsticks inside the bag and add some olive oil to it, coating it throughout. Once the chicken is coated with the olive oil, add in the spice mix made earlier, coating the chicken with the rub throughout. Once the drumsticks are nice and coated, shift the legs in the air fryer and let them cook for about 10 minutes. After 10 minutes flip the chicken and cook it for an additional 10 minutes. The chicken will be cooked once the internal temperature reaches around 165 degrees. Once done, serve with the sides or dips of desire.

Calories 223 Total Fat 12.4g Saturated Fat 2.4g Cholesterol 81mg Sodium 544mg Total Carbohydrate 1.7g Dietary Fiber 0.5g Total Sugars 0.5g Protein 25.7g

Air fried Lemon Feta Chicken(GF)

Prep: 15 Minutes | Cook Time: 25 Minutes | Makes: 2Servings

2 chicken breasts (skinless, halved)
1 tablespoon lemon juice
2 tablespoons feta cheese (crumbled)
½ teaspoon oregano (dried)
¼ teaspoon pepper

Begin by preheating the air fryer to around 400 degrees F. Grease a pan lightly and add the chicken to it. Pour over the lemon juice on the chicken and rub it all over, put some crumbled feta cheese over it, the oregano, and pepper. Place it in the air fryer and cook it for about 20 to 25 minutes or till the internal temperature reaches about 165 degrees F.

Calories 306 Total Fat 12.9 Saturated Fat 4.5g Cholesterol 138mg Sodium 232mg Total Carbohydrate 1g Dietary Fiber 0.3g Total Sugars 0.6g Protein 43.7g

Air Fired Greek Chicken (GF)

Prep: 15 Minutes | Cook Time: 15 Minutes | Makes: 2 Serving

1 chicken breast (boneless, skinless, about 10 ounces)
½ onions (coarsely chopped)
½ bell pepper (coarsely chopped)
½ zucchini (coarsely chopped)
1 teaspoon dried oregano
½ teaspoon parsley (dried)
½ teaspoon garlic powder
¼ teaspoon thyme (dried)
Salt and pepper (to taste)
1 ½ tablespoon olive oil (coconut or avocado oil can also be used)
2 tablespoons feta cheese (crumbled)

Begin by cutting the chicken to around 1-inch cubes. Add the chicken, bell pepper, onion, and zucchini to a bowl and mix them. Add the seasoning to the chicken bowl and drizzle some olive oil. Toss everything and give it a good mix till everything is well coated. Put this mixture in the air fryer and let it cook for about 15 minutes at around 380 degrees, making sure to shake the basket in between so the ingredients cook evenly throughout.
Once done, serve it on a serving plate with a garnish of feta cheese.

Calories 424 Total Fat 28.4g Saturated Fat 5.9g Cholesterol 88mg Sodium 281mg Total Carbohydrate 15.9g Dietary Fiber 4g Total Sugars 8.2g Protein 29.3g

Stuffed Chicken Breasts

Prep: 25 Minutes | Cook Time: 35Minutes | Makes: 4 Servings

2 tablespoons extra virgin olive oil
½ cup onion (diced)
½ cup bell pepper (diced)
½ cup mushrooms (diced)
1 teaspoon garlic (minced)
½ cup spinach (chopped)
½ teaspoon Italian seasoning (dried)
Salt and Pepper (to taste)
½ cup feta cheese (crumbled)
4 chicken breasts (boneless, skinless)
4 prosciutto slices
12 toothpicks
¾ cup Parmesan cheese (grated)
¾ cup dried bread crumbs
1 teaspoon parsley (dried)
1 teaspoon egg (beaten)
Cooking spray

Begin by heating the olive oil on a skillet over medium heat. Once the oil becomes hot, add in the chopped onion and cook them till they become soft which will take about 3 minutes. Then add the red bell pepper, and mushrooms, cooking them for another 3 minutes. Once they are cooked, tuner off the heat and add in the spinach, garlic, and seasoning of salt, Italian seasoning, and some pepper. Let the ingredients cook for a little more time, till the spinach becomes slightly wilted. Then stir in the feta cheese in the stuffing making sure to break up any crumbles into smaller pieces. Prepare the chicken by patting it dry using a paper towel and cutting pockets on the breasts using a knife and cutting the thickest part of the breast. Make sure not to cut the chicken breast all the way. Then preheat the air fryer to around 370 degrees F.

Put the prosciutto slices on a clean, flat, and prepped surface. Add about 2 tablespoons of the vegetable mixture prepared earlier and roll the slices around the filling. Tuck these prosciutto slices in the slits made on the breast earlier.

Mix parmesan cheese, breadcrumbs, parsley, salt, and pepper in a tray and coat the chicken with it and then drench the breast in some beaten egg, and then coat another layer of breadcrumbs on the chicken. Put this coated chicken in the air fryer and cook it for about 22 minutes or till the crust becomes golden brown and the internal temperature reaches at least 165 degrees.

Calories 565 Total Fat 22.1g Saturated Fat 8.4g Cholesterol 200mg Sodium 1561mg Total Carbohydrate 20g Dietary Fiber 1.6g Total Sugars 3.6g Protein 68g

Greek Chicken Skewers with Feta cheese Sauce

Prep: 15 Minutes | Cook Time: 8 Minutes | Makes: 2Servings

3 chicken breasts (boneless, sliced to bite-sized pieces)
2 lemons
2 garlic cloves (minced)
2 tablespoon Greek yogurt
2 tablespoon olive oil
1 tablespoon oregano (dried)
1 teaspoon thyme (dried)
Salt and Pepper (to taste)

For Feta Sauce:
3 oz. feta cheese (crumbled)
3 tablespoon Greek yogurt
½ lemon (zested, juiced)
1 garlic clove (minced)
1 teaspoon oregano (chopped)
½ teaspoon red pepper flakes (crushed)
Black pepper (to taste)

Take a large bowl and mix lemon juice and its zest, yogurt, garlic, oregano, thyme, olive oil, and salt and pepper, to make the marinade for the chicken. Put the chickens inside the marinade and toss to cover the chicken pieces throughout, leaving them in the marinade for at least 2 hours or if time is available, overnight. For the Feta cheese sauce, take all the ingredients for the sauce and add them to the food processor, pulsing the processor till all the ingredients become well combined and smooth. Slice the whole lemons into small wedges and thread them on a skewer, interchanging with the chicken, while making the skewers make sure they fit inside the air fryer. Heat the air fryer to about 350 degrees and let the skewers cook for about 8 minutes. Once done, take them out and serve them on a serving plate with the side of the dipping sauce made earlier.

Calories 831 Total Fat 43.9g Saturated Fat 16g Cholesterol 243mg Sodium 731mg Total Carbohydrate 18.3g Dietary Fiber 3g Total Sugars 11.4g Protein 90.8g

Grilled Chicken Kabobs (GF)

Prep: 25 Minutes | Cook Time: 15 Minutes | Makes: 2 Servings

1 pound Chicken Breasts
2 teaspoon Garlic Puree
1 lemon juice and rind
2 teaspoon Extra virgin olive oil
2 teaspoon thyme
2 teaspoon oregano
Salt and Pepper (or to taste)

Begin by dicing the kabobs into medium-sized pieces. Add all the ingredients to a bowl and give it a good mix with the hands. Add the chicken to the mixture and cover it up with the siren wrap. Let the chicken stay in the marinade for a few hours. Once the chicken has rested in the marinade for a good amount of time, remove it from the marinade and put it in the air fryer cooking the chicken for about 15 minutes at around 375 degrees F.

Calories 486 Total Fat 22.7g Saturated Fat 5.4g Cholesterol 202mg Sodium 221mg Total Carbohydrate 1.6g Dietary Fiber 1g Total Sugars 0.1g Protein 65.9g

Greek Chicken and Orzo Pasta Salad

Prep: 15 Minutes | Cook Time: 15 Minutes | Makes: 4 Servings

2 tablespoons olive oil
1 teaspoon Kosher Salt
½ teaspoon Oregano (or to taste)
½ teaspoon garlic powder
¼ teaspoon black pepper
1 lemon's juice
1 pound chicken tenderloins (boneless, skinless)
2 tablespoon butter (unsalted)
1 tablespoon extra-virgin olive oil
1 garlic clove (minced)
½ cup breadcrumbs

Dressing:
½ cup extra virgin olive oil
¼ cup red wine vinegar
1 teaspoon kosher salt
½ teaspoon oregano (dried)
½ teaspoon black pepper (grounded)
1 garlic clove (grated)
½ lemon's juice

Salad:
Kosher salt
1 pound orzo
10 ounces grape tomatoes (halved)
1 English cucumber (diced)
¼ cup parsley
1 ½ cup feta cheese (crumbled)

For the chicken:

Take a medium bowl and mix the salt, olive oil, garlic powder, oregano, pepper, and lemon juice. Add in the chicken and give everything a good mix so the chicken is coated throughout, letting the chicken rest for about 30 mins or 4 hours if time is available. Then preheat the air fryer to 400 degrees F. Take the chicken out of the marinade and put it on the basket of air fryers for cooking it for about 5 minutes on each side. Once each side has been heated, take it off the grill and slice it to about 1-inch pieces after letting it rest for some time.

For the breadcrumbs:

Take a medium skillet and add the butter, olive oil, and garlic in it, heating everything over low heat. Once the garlic begins to sizzle, add in the breadcrumbs and put them into the oven to make them crispy. Let them stay in the air fryer for about 3 minutes, or until the breadcrumbs turn golden brown.

For the dressing:

Take a bowl and mix all the ingredients for the dressing.

For the salad:

Boil some salted water in a large bowl and add the orzo till they are cooked, once done drain them out and add them to the large serving bowl. Add in the dressing as it is hot and let everything cool down at room temperature. Once everything is cooled off, add in the tomatoes, cucumber, and parsley, making sure to mix everything, top everything off with some feta cheese, the chicken cooked earlier, and the breadcrumbs.

Calories 861 Total Fat 28.4g Saturated Fat 13.3g Cholesterol 114mg Sodium 1574mg
Total Carbohydrate 102.6g Dietary Fiber 6.1g Total Sugars 12.5g Protein 48.1g

Spinach and Feta Stuffed Chicken Breasts

Prep: 15 Minutes | Cook Time: 25 Minutes | Makes: 2Servings

2 chicken breasts
6 oz. spinach
½ cup Feta cheese (crumbled)
1 garlic clove (minced)
Salt and Pepper (to taste)
¼ teaspoon salt
2 tablespoon avocado oil
¼ cup onion (chopped)

Take a medium skillet and heat up some oil in it over medium heat, add the spinach to the heated oil and let it sauté for about 3 minutes. Add some garlic, salt, and onion to the pan with spinach. Let everything sauté for about 3 more minutes, removing everything from the pan and then shifting it to a bowl. Add some feta cheese to the spinach mix and mix everything. Take the chicken and slice about 4-inch cuts on the breast of the chicken. Spoon about ½ tablespoon of the mix and stuff it in the slits made before. Close the slits using some toothpicks and sprinkle them with some garlic powder and salt. Drizzle some avocado oil and massage it on the chicken, putting it on the air fryer cooking it for about 25 minutes at 177°C (350°F).

The chicken will be done and ready to serve once the internal temperature of the chicken becomes at least 75°C (165°F).

Calories 486 Total Fat 22.7g Saturated Fat 5.4g Cholesterol 202mg
Sodium 221mg Total Carbohydrate 1.6g Dietary Fiber 1g
Total Sugars 0.1g Protein 65.9g

Mediterranean Chicken thighs

Prep: 15 Minutes | Cook Time: 25 Minutes | Makes: 4 Servings

2- 1 pound chicken thighs (bone-in, skin-on)
½ cup extra virgin olive oil
2 tablespoon red wine vinegar
1 lemon's juice and zest
4 garlic cloves (minced)
2 teaspoon oregano
½ teaspoon thyme
1 teaspoon paprika
1 teaspoon cumin
¼ teaspoon cayenne pepper
1 teaspoon salt (or to taste)
1/8 teaspoon black pepper
Parsley (for garnish)
Feta cheese (for garnish)

For Salad:
3 tomatoes (seeded, diced)
½ English cucumber (diced)
5 green onion
¼ cup Parsley (chopped)
¼ Feta cheese (crumbled)
¼ cup extra virgin olive oil
½ lemon's juice
2 cloves garlic (minced)
1 teaspoon sumac
Salt and Pepper (or to taste)

Begin by preparing the chicken, trimming the extra fat, and patting it dry using a paper towel. Add some lemon zest and juice, garlic cloves, olive oil, oregano, thyme, cumin, paprika, and cayenne pepper in a bowl for the marinade, giving everything a good mix until everything is well combined. Once everything is combined, take a ziplock bag and add the prepared chicken in it, add the marinade mix all over the chicken, and massage it all over it, letting the chicken rest in the marinade sauce for at least 2 hours inside a fridge. Once the chicken has rested for a good amount of time in the fridge, take it out letting it rest at room temperature, meanwhile heat the air fryer to about 193°C (380°F). Grease the basket of the air fryer with a little bit of oil and add the chicken inside the basket, skin side down, and cook it for about 10 minutes with the skin down, and then for another 15 minutes with the skin side up. Let the chicken cook until its internal temperature reaches about 75°C (165°F). Meanwhile, mix all the ingredients for the salad in a bowl and set it at the bottom of the platter layering the chicken on top of the salad bed. Give the dish a garnish of parsley and feta cheese and serve.

Calories 787 Total Fat 50.6g Saturated Fat 13.9g Cholesterol 235mg Sodium 1206mg Total Carbohydrate 10.2g Dietary Fibre 2.6g Total Sugars 5.2g Protein 72.8g

Greek Chicken bowl

Prep: 15 Minutes | Cook Time: 12 Minutes | Makes: 2 Servings

1 recipe air fried chicken breasts
1 recipe instant pot quinoa
4 cucumber tomato salad servings
¼ cup feta cheese
½ cup kalamata olives
1 lemon vinaigrette dressing recipe

Grease air fryer basket with oil spray. Cook chicken breast in it for 12 minutes, flipping halfway at 204°C (400°F). Begin by dividing all the ingredients into 4 bowls. Add the dressing on top and give it a good mix, and the chicken bowl will be ready to serve. The chicken bowl can be stored for some time if made in an air-tight container.

Calories 574 Total Fat 32.2g Saturated Fat 4.9g Cholesterol 71mg Sodium 1411mg Total Carbohydrate 36.9g Dietary Fibre 4.6g Total Sugars 2.8g Protein 32.7g

Turkey Panini

Prep: 15 Minutes | Cook Time: 15 Minutes | Makes: 2Servings

10 bacon strips
3 white bread slices
¼ cup ranch dressing
10 Ounce turkey breasts
4 American cheese slices
2 teaspoon butter (salted)

Begin by layering the bacon strips on an airflow rack and place that rack inside the air fryer, cooking them for about 15 minutes at around 400 degrees, making sure to rotate them halfway. When done, take out the bacon strips from the fryer and let them rest for later use. Take the bread slices and add butter on one side of it, putting them in the air fryer with the airflow. Put the turkey breast, cheese, and cooked bacon on top. Close the sandwich by adding another buttered slice on top of everything, and then cook everything in the air fryer for about 10 minutes.
Serve with ranch

Calories 865 Total Fat 62.3g Saturated Fat 24.2g Cholesterol 105mg Sodium 3758mg Total Carbohydrate 17.7g Dietary Fiber 1.1g Total Sugars 9.5g Protein 53.4g

Mini Greek-Style Meat loves and Arugula Salad

Prep: 15 Minutes | Cook Time: 20 Minutes | Makes: 2Servings

8 ounces ground beef
6-ounce ground lamb
½ cup breadcrumbs
½ cup onions
4 teaspoon mint leaves
4 teaspoon thyme
1 teaspoon salt
¼ teaspoon mixed spice
¼ teaspoon red pepper (crushed)
3 garlic cloves (crushed)
1 egg
Cooking spray
1 cup Greek Yogurt
3-ounce Feta cheese
1 tablespoon mint and thyme
2 tablespoon lemon juice
1 tablespoon extra-virgin olive oil
1 teaspoon black pepper
4 cups arugula leaves
2 cups cucumber

Begin by preheating up the air fryer to about 204°C (400°F).
In a mixing bowl, add the first 4 ingredients and give them a good mix, once everything is mixed add in the thyme, mixed spice, salt, red pepper, eggs, and garlic. Grease some cups and add the mixture to them. Put these cups inside of an air fryer and let them cook for about 20 minutes. at 204°C (400°F). Meanwhile, take a blender and blend the feta cheese, lemon juice, mint, yogurt, and thyme until they turn into a smooth mix. Add some oil, salt, and pepper along with some of the rocket leaves and mix everything up to make the salad. For serving, add the meatloaf on top of the bed of argula salad finishing it off with the dressing made earlier.

Calories 819 Total Fat 36.1g Saturated Fat 15.1g Cholesterol 303mg Sodium 2065mg Total Carbohydrate 38.5g Dietary Fibre 4.6g Total Sugars 12.6g Protein 83.8g

Lamb chops with Lemon thyme, and Farro Vinaigrette

Prep: 15 Minutes | Cook Time: 8 Minutes | Makes: 2Servings

Cooking spray
9 lamb chops

Salt and Pepper (to taste)
1 teaspoon lemon zest
2 tablespoon lemon juice
2 tablespoon extra-virgin olive oil
1 tablespoon shallots
2 teaspoon honey
1 teaspoon Dijon mustard
½ cup precooked Farro
2 ounces arugula

Begin by greasing the basket of airfare with some cooking spray
Add the lamb chops to the air fryer basket and cook it for about 8 minutes, making sure to flip the lamb while it is cooking.
While the lamb is cooking, take a bowl and mix the next 7 ingredients with the seasoning of salt and pepper.
Once everything is cooked, add in the arugula leaves and faro, mixing everything by tossing.
Once done, serve all together.

Calories 580 Total Fat 28.3g Saturated Fat 8.1g Cholesterol 230mg Sodium 221mg Total Carbohydrate 5.6g Dietary Fiber 0.5g Total Sugars 4.5g Protein 72.4g

Beef and Lamb Kofta Lettuce Wraps

Prep: 15 Minutes | Cook Time: 10 Minutes | Makes: 2Servings

2 bread slices (crumbled)
7 ounces ground beef
5 tablespoons onion
2 tablespoon parsley
5 ounces ground lamb
1 tablespoon mint
½ teaspoon cinnamon powder
½ teaspoon allspice powder
1 egg
Salt and Pepper (to taste)
1 tablespoon olive oil
1 cup Greek yogurt
3 tablespoon cucumber
2 tablespoon onions (chopped)
1 brown rice pack (precooked)
1 teaspoon paprika powder
2 tablespoons vegetable oil
10 lettuce leaves

Begin by crumbling up the breadcrumbs using a food processor.
Mix the freshly made crumbs, onions, parsley, beef, lamb, and the next five ingredients in a mixing bowl, once everything is well mixed, make around 8 patties using the mixture. Put these patties in an air fryer basket and cook for 5 minutes on each side While the patties are cooking, mix the yogurt, salt, pepper, cucumber, onions in a bowl. Prepare the brown rice according to the packaging instruction and add some oil and paprika to the cooked rice. Once the patties are done, serve the dish with some lettuce leaves on the bottom, adding the rice on top, then the yogurt, topping everything off with the patty.

Calories 989 Total Fat 39.2g Saturated Fat 10.6g Cholesterol 239mg Sodium 253mg Total Carbohydrate 85.1g Detary Fibre 4.5g Total Sugars 6.1g Protein 71.3g

Roast Lamb with Mint Sauce Glaze

Prep: 15 Minutes | Cook Time: 20 Minutes | Makes: 4 Servings

3 pounds Boneless Lamb leg
3 garlic cloves
2 tablespoon olive oil
½ teaspoon sea salt
¼ teaspoon cracked Pepper

For mint sauce glaze
½ cup mint leaves (chopped finely)
2 tablespoon brown sugar
2 ½ tablespoon Malt vinegar
2 tablespoon Boiling water
1 teaspoon salt

Begin by pat drying the lamb using a paper towel and cutting around 1-inch cuts along the skin. Cut the garlic into slivers and put them in the slits made using a sharp knife. Drizzle some olive oil on top of the lamb leg and massage it all over it, making sure to cover all corners, once the leg is coated fully by oil add a generous amount of sea salt and fresh cracked black pepper. Heat the air fryer to around 180°C (355°F) and put the lamb inside the basket, letting it cook for about 20 minutes. Meanwhile, add some boiling water, brown sugar, and salt to a mixing bowl and mix everything until they become a homogenous mixture. Then add in the mint leaves, and malt vinegar. Once the lamb has cooked for 5 minutes, baste the leg with the mint glaze and let it cook for another 15 minutes. Keep basting the lamb after every 5 minutes until the lamb meat reaches desired consistency. Once the lamb is done, wrap it with some aluminium foil and let it sit for about 10 minutes before carving and serving.

Calories 870 Total Fat 64.3g Saturated Fat 25.1g Cholesterol 241mg Sodium 1017mg Total Carbohydrate 6.2g Dietary Fibre 0.8g Total Sugars 4.4g Protein 60.7g

Pistachio Crusted Lamb Rack

Prep: 15 Minutes | Cook Time: 19 Minutes | Makes: 4 Servings

1 lamb rack (trimmed and frenched, 7x7 inch)
1 teaspoon kosher salt
¼ teaspoon pepper
1/3 cup pistachios (finely chopped)
2 tablespoon breadcrumbs
1 teaspoon rosemary (chopped finely)
2 teaspoon thyme (chopped finely)
1 tablespoon butter (melted)
1 tablespoon Dijon

Begin by inserting the split in the rack to the meaty side of the ribs, which will be next to the bone. If required, use a pointed metal skewer and make the first hole. Then put in the rotisserie forks on either side and tighten the knobs so the rack is held firmly, make sure to season the rack generously with some salt and pepper. Put the drip pan at the bottom and cook the meat for about 12 minutes at around 380 degrees. While it is cooking, mix the pistachios, breadcrumbs and the herbs in a bowl, once they all are thoroughly mixed, add in the butter and toss it. When the meat is done, take it out of the rack and spread the Dijon on the meaty side of the lamb, and rub the chopped pistachio mixture on it. Put the meaty side back on the basket of the air fryer and let it cook for another 7 minutes.

The meat will be ready to serve once the internal temperature reaches around 140 degrees.

Calories 220 Total Fat 11.5g Saturated Fat 4.3g Cholesterol 81mg Sodium 716mg Total Carbohydrate 4.4g Dietary Fiber 1g 4% Total Sugars 0.6g Protein 24.5g

Garlic and Rosemary Lamb Chops

Prep: 15 Minutes | Cook Time: 8 Minutes | Makes: 3 Servings

2 pound Lamb loin chops
4 teaspoon garlic (minced)
1 tablespoon rosemary
1 teaspoon lemon zest
1 tablespoon of lemon juice
2 tablespoon olive oil
1 teaspoon salt
½ teaspoon black pepper

Start by mixing olive oil, garlic, lemon juice and zest, salt, pepper, and rosemary in a bowl, once they are properly mixed, add them over to the lamb chops and rub them around them, making sure to coat all the surface. Let the lamb chops rest with the marinade for at least 1 hour, making sure to cove the lamb chops with saran wrap. Once the lamb chops have been resting in the marinade for a good amount of time, take them out and cook them in the air fryer for about 8-12 minutes at 204°C (400°F)., flipping halfway.

Calories 653 Total Fat 31.7g Saturated Fat 9.3g Cholesterol 272mg Sodium 1006mg Total Carbohydrate 2.3g Dietary Fibre 0.7g Total Sugars 0.1g Protein 85.3g

Lamb chops with Dijon Garlic Marinade

Prep: 15 Minutes | Cook Time: 14 Minutes | Makes: 4 Servings

2 teaspoon Dijon mustard
2 teaspoon olive oil
1 teaspoon soy sauce
1 teaspoon garlic (minced)
1 teaspoon cumin powder
1 teaspoon cayenne pepper
1 teaspoon Italian spice blend
(optional)
¼ teaspoon salt
8 lamb chops

Start by making the marinade for the lamb chops. To make the marinade take a mixing bowl and mix the Dijon mustard, soy sauce, garlic, olive oil, cumin powder, cayenne pepper, salt, and the Italian spice blend thoroughly. For marinating the chops, put the lambs inside of a ziplock bag and pour the marinade all over them, massage the marinade onto the marinade thoroughly until the chops are thoroughly covered. Let the lamb chops rest inside the fridge for at least 30 minutes, if there is time, let them stay in the marinade overnight. Preheat the air fryer and put the lamb chops on it, letting them cook for about 14 minutes at around 193°C (380°F), flipping them halfway, and cooking for the remaining time. Once done, take the lamb chops out of the air fryer and give it a garnish of cumin and some extra salt.

Calories 343 Total Fat 15.1g Saturated Fat 4.8g Cholesterol 153mg Sodium 381mg Total Carbohydrate 0.9g Dietary Fibre 0.3g Total Sugars 0.1g Protein 48.1g

Quick Kofta

Prep: 15 Minutes | Cook Time: 8 Minutes | Makes: 4 Servings

½ cup onion
½ cup breadcrumbs
¼ cup mint
½ teaspoon salt
1 teaspoon garlic (crushed)
2 tablespoon tomato paste
½ teaspoon cumin
¼ teaspoon cinnamon
¼ teaspoon red pepper
¼ teaspoon allspice powder
1 pound grounded beef
1 egg
Cooking spray
10 tomato plum slices
4 pita bread
¼ cup yogurt

Mix the first 12 ingredients in a bowl and mix the ingredients thoroughly. From the mixed mixture make about 8 circular patties form it. Then spray some cooking spray on a pan and let the patties cook inside air fryer for about 8 minutes making sure to flip them halfway in the cooking process. Serve with pitta bread and yogurt.

Calories 497 Total Fat 11.9g Saturated Fat 4.7g Cholesterol 143mg Sodium 850mg Total Carbohydrate 51.4g Dietary Fibre 3.9g Total Sugars 4.8g Protein 44g

Lamb Chops With Orange Butter (GF)

Prep: 15 Minutes | Cook Time: 12 Minutes | Makes: 2 Servings

2 tablespoon butter (softened)
1 tablespoon orange marmalade
¼ teaspoon marjoram leaves (dried)
2 lamb shoulders chops
¼ teaspoon paprika
¼ teaspoon black and red pepper blend

Begin by preheating the contact grill. Take a small bowl and mix the butter, marjoram, and marmalade, once mixed set it aside for later use. Coat the lamb chops with some seasoning of salt, paprika, and pepper blend. Put the coated lamb on to air fryer basket or rack and cook it for about 8 to 12 minutes or until the meat reaches the desired doneness. Once the lamb is cooked to the required doneness, serve it on a serving plate with a little of the butter made earlier.

Calories 298 Total Fat 20.6g Saturated Fat 10.3g Cholesterol 106mg Sodium 168mg Total Carbohydrate 7g Dietary Fibre 0.3g Total Sugars 6g Protein 22.2g

Skirt Steak with Balsamic Shallots (GF) (DF)

Prep: 15 Minutes | Cook Time: 12 Minutes | Makes: 2 Servings

¼ cup balsamic vinegar
2 teaspoon Brown sugar
Salt and Pepper (to taste)
2 garlic cloves (chopped)
½ olive oil
1 pound Skirt steak
10 shallots (peeled)

Begin by mixing all the ingredients required for the marinade inside a mixing bowl and put the steak and shallots in it for at least 30 mins. Once both the ingredients have been resting in the marinade for a decent amount of time, take them out and shift them to an airflow rack. Let the meat cook for about 15 minutes at around 204°C (400°F), inside the air fryer, making sure to flip it halfway. Once the steak has reached the desired doneness, take it out of the air fryer and let it rest for at least 10 minutes before slicing and serving.

Calories 298 Total Fat 20.6g Saturated Fat 10.3g Cholesterol 106mg Sodium 168mg Total Carbohydrate 7g Dietary Fibre 0.3g Total Sugars 6g Protein 22.2g

Orange Balsamic Lamb chops(GF) (DF)

Prep: 15 Minutes | Cook Time: 12 Minutes | Makes: 4 Servings

4 teaspoon olive oil
2 tablespoon lemon juice
2 teaspoon orange zest
1 tablespoon orange juice
6 lamb chops
Salt and Pepper (to taste)
4 tablespoon Balsamic Vinegar
Cooking spray

Begin by mixing the oil, lemon juice, and lamb chops in a bowl and mix them well. Let it rest for 5 minutes, and then add in the salt and pepper. Grease the air fryer basket with some cooking spray and put the lamb in it, then cook for about 12 minutes, flipping halfway through. While the lamb is cooking, add vinegar, orange juice, and orange zest to a pot and bring everything to a boil. When the vinegar has thickened, turn off the heat. Once the lamb has reached the desired doneness, serve them on a serving plate with a drizzle of the vinegar syrup.

Calories 961 Total Fat 40.8g Saturated Fat 13.6g Cholesterol 441mg Sodium 375mg Total Carbohydrate 1g Dietary Fibre 0.2g Total Sugars 0.6g Protein 137.8g

Mediterranean Ribeye (GF)

Prep: 25 Minutes | Cook Time: 70 Minutes | Makes: 2 Servings

4 garlic cloves (minced)
½ teaspoon salt
¼ teaspoon pepper
2 beef ribeye steaks
3 tablespoons basil (chopped)
1 tablespoon oregano (minced)
2 teaspoon olive oil
2 teaspoon lemon juice
2 tablespoon feta cheese (crumbled)
Kalamata olive and lemon wedges (optional)

Take a pot and add some water to it, heating it to exactly 110 degrees. This water will be used to cook the steak using the sous vide method. While the water is heating, coat the steak with some salt pepper, and a bit of crushed garlic. Add the herbs to the garlic and rub it on the steak. Put these seasoned steaks in a ziplock bag and try to remove as much air as possible. Once most of the air has been removed place it in the water and cover the pot with a glass lid, letting the steak cook for 1 hour (the steak may look under cooked). Once the steak has been cooking for one hour, take it out of the water and wipe dry all the excess water. Put an airflow rack inside the air fryer and place the steak pieces on top of it. Drizzle some olive oil on top of it and let the air fryer cook the steak for about 10 minutes at 390 degrees F.

Once the internal temperature of the steak reaches 140 degrees F, take it out of the air fryer and serve it with a little drizzle of lemon juice and garnish of cheese. The steak can also be topped with some olive and served with the side of lemon wedges.

Calories 241 Total Fat 13.2g Saturated Fat 4.7g Cholesterol 63mg Sodium 708mg Total Carbohydrate 4.3g Dietary Fibre 1.3g Total Sugars 0.7g Protein 2.2g

Air fried Steak Kebabs (GF)

Prep: 15 Minutes | Cook Time: 12 Minutes | Makes: 2 Servings

1 pound sirloin steak (cut to 1 inch chunks)
¼ cup olive oil
¼ cup soy sauce
1 tablespoon garlic (minced)
1 teaspoon brown sugar
½ teaspoon cumin (grounded)
¼ teaspoon black pepper
8 oz. Baby Bella mushrooms (stems removed)
1 onion (chopped to 1-inch pieces)
1 green bell pepper (chopped to 1-inch pieces)
Salt and Pepper (to taste)

Mix the steak pieces with the oil, soy sauce, garlic, brown sugar, cumin, salt, and black pepper. Let the steak chunks marinate in the marinade for at least 30 minutes, if time is available, let it stay in the marinade for a little longer. Once the steak has been resting in the marinade for a good amount of time, take it out and thread it through a skewer with the Bella mushrooms, green peppers, and onions. Heat the air fryer to around 390 degrees F and put the skewers inside it, cooking everything for around 10 to 12 minutes.

Calories 739 Total Fat 39.9g Saturated Fat 9g Cholesterol 203mg Sodium 1959mg Total Carbohydrate 21.1g Dietary Fibre 4.2g Total Sugars 9.4g Protein 75.2g

Mediterranean Beef Pitas with yogurt-cucumber Salad (GF)

Prep: 15 Minutes | Cook Time: 12 Minutes | Makes: 2 Servings

2-pound beef steak
2 cups yogurt
1 tablespoon lemon juice
1 tablespoon garlic (crushed)
1 cucumber
Salt and Pepper (to taste)
6 pita bread
¾ cup hummus
10 cherry tomatoes
3 tablespoon Feta cheese

Begin by mixing 1 cup yogurt, garlic, and lemon in a mixing bowl. Once all the ingredients are mixed, add the steak to it and let it rest in the marinade for at least 6 hours. While the steak is resting in the yogurt mixture, take the vegetables and begin slicing them lengthwise, taking the sliced cucumber and adding it to the yogurt mix. Then add in a bit of sea salt and pepper, refrigerate it for another few hours. Once the steak is well-rested in the marinade, take it out and cook in the air fryer for about 12 minutes at 204°C (400°F). Spread the hummus over the pitta bread and add some cucumbers, tomatoes, and beefsteak on top. The pitta bread can be served as is, or some more toppings can also be added to them.

Calories 1846 Total Fat 46.9g Saturated Fat 17.2g Cholesterol 433mg Sodium 1982mg Total Carbohydrate 162.5g Dietary Fiber 17.9g Total Sugars 39.1g Protein 184.1g

Roasted Lamb Rack With Lemon Cumin Crust(GF)

Prep: 15 Minutes | Cook Time: 25 Minutes | Makes: 3Servings

1.7 pound frenched Rack of lamb
Salt and Pepper (to taste)
3 ounces breadcrumbs (sourdough)
1 teaspoon garlic (grated)
½ teaspoon salt
1 teaspoon cumin seeds
1 teaspoon ground cumin
Grated lemon rind
1 egg (beaten)

Begin by preheating the air fryer at 175°C (350°F). Season the lamb generously with some black pepper and some salt. Mix the grated garlic, breadcrumbs, ½ teaspoon salt, cumin seeds, ground cumin, oil, and lemon rinds in a large bowl, whisk the eggs in another bowl and begin coating the lamb rack. To coat the lamb rack, first, drench the lamb with eggs and then give it a nice coat of the breadcrumb mix. Put the coated lamb into the air fryer and let it cook for about 20 minutes. After the 20 minutes is up increase the temperature to 200°C (390°F), letting it cook for another 5 minutes. Once done, take it out of the air fryer and cover it with foil, letting it rest for about 10 minutes before serving.

Calories 579 Total Fat 28.4g Saturated Fat 11.1g Cholesterol 227mg Sodium 778mg Total Carbohydrate 23g Dietary Fibre 1.9g Total Sugars 2.4g Protein 56.5g

Cabbage and Beef Rolls

Prep: 15 Minutes | Cook Time: 10 Minutes | Makes: 2 Servings

10 egg roll wrappers
1 pound corned beef, shredded
1.5 cups stewed cabbage
1/3 cup of Spicy Mustard
Oil spray, for greasing

Combine the corned beef and cabbage in a bowl. Put the egg roll wrapper on a flat surface. Add bowl mixture onto the corner of the wrapper, and roll it, by brushing the edges with water then seal the rolls. Grease the roll with oil spray. Put the rolls in the air fryer basket. Adjust the time to 10 minutes at 200°C (390°F). Once it's done, serve with spicy mustard.

Calories 853 Total Fat 31g Saturated Fat 12.6g Cholesterol 156mg Sodium 2920mg Total Carbohydrate 92.6g Dietary Fibre 2.9g Total Sugars 0g Protein 46.1g

Stuffed Mozzarella Patties

Prep: 15 Minutes | Cook Time: 8 Minutes | Makes: 2 Servings

10 egg roll wrappers
1 pound corned beef, shredded
1.5 cups stewed cabbage
1/3 cup of Spicy Mustard
Oil spray, for greasing

Cut the mozzarella cheese into pieces. Place two pepperonis over the cheese slices. Then add other cheese slices on top forming a sandwich, seal it slightly. To seal it: In a large bowl mix plain breadcrumbs, panko breadcrumbs, and Italian seasoning. Whisk eggs in a separate bowl. Dump the cheese patties in egg mixture and then dredge into the breadcrumbs. Mist it with oil spray. Place it inside the air fryer basket. Adjust the temperature at 204°C (400°F), for 8 minutes, flipping halfway through. Once it's done, Serve.

Calories 1319 Total Fat 64.3g Saturated Fat 19.7g Cholesterol 593mg Sodium 3393mg Total Carbohydrate 117.9g Dietary Fibre 6.8g Total Sugars 11.6g Protein 60.6g

Steak with Balsamic Shallots (GF)

Prep: 15 Minutes | Cook Time: 25 Minutes | Makes: 3Servings

Marinade Ingredients

1/3 cup balsamic vinegar
1 teaspoon Brown Sugar
Salt and black pepper, to taste
3 cloves garlic, chopped
½ teaspoon of Olive Oil

Steak Ingredients

1 .2 pound skirt steak
4 shallots, peeled

Combine all the marinade ingredients in a bowl. Marinate the steak and shallots in it for 60 minutes in a refrigerator. Take out both and arrange them inside the air fryer Press the steak button and set the timer to 20 minutes at 200 degrees F, flipping it halfway through. Take it out and let it get cool for 10 minutes, before serving.

Calories 480 Total Fat 23.6g Saturated Fat 8.8g Cholesterol 134mg Sodium 173mg Total Carbohydrate 2g Dietary Fibre 0.1g Total Sugars 1g Protein 60.7g

Air Fry Loin Lamb Chops

Prep: 12 Minutes | Cook Time: 15 Minutes | Makes: 2 Servings

4 clove Garlic, sliced
1 tablespoon minced rosemary leaves
2 teaspoons Red Wine Vinegar
2 tablespoons Soy sauce
3 tablespoons Olive oil
6-8 loin lamb chops, 1 ½ in. thick

In a large mixing bowl, combine rosemary leaves, garlic, red wine vinegar, soy sauce, and olive oil. Marinade the lamb chop in it for 3 hours in the refrigerator. Then put the chops on the air fryer and set the timer to 15 minutes at 185°C (370°F). Rotate the chops after 7 minutes of cooking. Once done, serve.

Calories 1164 Total Fat 99.3g Saturated Fat 36.1g Cholesterol 240mg Sodium 1099mg Total Carbohydrate 4.3g Dietary Fibre 1g Total Sugars 0.4g Protein 58.5g

Air Fried Pumpkin seeds (GF)

Prep: 15 Minutes | Cook Time: 15 Minutes | Makes: 2 Servings

2 pumpkin seeds
1 ½ tablespoon butter
½ teaspoon garlic salt

Begin by taking out the seeds from the pumpkin and cleaning them off by putting them under running water. Put a large pot of water on the stove and bring it to a boil, once the water starts boiling add in the pumpkin seeds and boil them for 5 minutes, and then drain them. After draining them, add them to the butter and garlic salt mixture and toss it around to coat. When all the seeds are fully coated, put them in the air fryer, cooking them for about 15 minutes at 182°C (360°F), making sure to shake them halfway.

Calories 825 Total Fat 71.9g Saturated Fat 17.4g Cholesterol 23mg Sodium 86mg Total Carbohydrate 25.1g Dietary Fibre 5.5g Total Sugars 1.6g Protein 34.1g

Avocado and Egg Pizza Toast (GF)

Prep: 15 Minutes | Cook Time: 10 Minutes | Makes: 2 Servings

4 bread pieces (sides trimmed)
3 eggs
1 avocado (sliced thinly)
1/5 cup mayo
½ cup cheddar cheese (shredded)
¼ cup Mozzarella Cheese (shredded)
Salt and Pepper (to taste)

Begin by preheating the air fryer to around 400 degrees F. Drizzle a little bit of oil on a springform pan, and line it with bread such that the entire bottom of the pan is covered with the bread. Add about ¾ of the mayo on the bread and ¾ of the cheddar cheese. Set the avocado slices along the edges of the pan and then fill in the center as well, when done properly, there are three compartments created where the eggs can be cracked. Crack the egg in each of the compartments and add the remaining mayo on top. Put the remaining cheese over the slices and put it in the preheated air fryer and keep it there till the cheese melts. When the cheese melts, turn the heat of the air fryer to 350 degrees F and let it cook for 6 minutes. Then sprinkle some more mozzarella cheese and put it in the air fryer for another 2 to 3 minutes, and make sure that the egg is cooked throughout.

Calories 648 Total Fat 45.7g Saturated Fat 14g Cholesterol 283mg Sodium 803mg Total Carbohydrate 40.6g Dietary Fiber 7.9g Total Sugars 4.8g Protein 22.3g

Dry Rub Chicken (GF)

Prep: 15 Minutes | Cook Time: 12 Minutes | Makes: 4 Servings

4 chicken thighs (skin on, bone-in)
2 tablespoon olive oil
1 tablespoon Italian seasoning
2 teaspoon paprika
2 teaspoon garlic powder
2 teaspoon onion powder
½ teaspoon salt
½ teaspoon black pepper

Begin by mixing all the dry ingredient in a bowl and setting it aside. Make a few slits on the flesh of the chicken, making sure not to cut through it. Then dry the chicken by patting it down using a paper towel. Once the chicken is dry, rub some olive oil on both of the sides of the chicken and then add the dry rub made earlier to the chicken. Line the air fryer basket with some foil and grease it lightly. Put the chicken in the air fryer basket, making sure not to stack them, and bake it at around 360 degrees F for around 8 minutes, and then increase the temperature to 400 degrees F, cooking it for further 4 minutes. The chicken will be cooked and ready to serve once the internal temperature reaches around 165 degrees F.

Calories 361 Total Fat 19g Saturated Fat 4.2g Cholesterol 132mg Sodium 419mg Total Carbohydrate 3.1g Dietary Fiber 0.7g Total Sugars 1.2g Protein 42.8g

Garlic and Herb Artisan Bread

Prep: 15 Minutes | Cook Time: 12 Minutes | Makes: 2Servings

1 cup water
½ tablespoon instant yeast
½ tablespoon salt
1 cup all-purpose flour
2 teaspoon garlic powder
½ teaspoon onion powder
1 teaspoon thyme
½ teaspoon dried parsley

Begin by preheating the air fryer to around 204°C (400°F). Drizzle a little bit of oil on a springform pan, and line it with bread such that the entire bottom of the pan is covered with the bread. Add about ¾ of the mayo on the bread and ¾ of the Cheddar cheese. Set the avocado slices along the edges of the pan and then fill in the center as well, when done properly, there are three compartments created where the eggs can be cracked. Crack the egg in each of the compartments and add the remaining mayo on top. Put the remaining cheese over the slices and put it in the preheated air fryer and keep it there until the cheese melts. When the cheese melts, turn the heat of the air fryer to 177°C (350°F) and let it cook for 6 minutes. Then sprinkle some more mozzarella cheese and put it in the air fryer for another 2 to 3 minutes, and make sure that the egg is cooked throughout.

Calories 648 Total Fat 45.7g Saturated Fat 14g Cholesterol 283mg Sodium 803mg Total Carbohydrate 40.6g Dietary Fibre 7.9g Total Sugars 4.8g Protein 22.3g

Foil Wrapped Sausage and Potatoes

Prep: 15 Minutes | Cook Time: 18 Minutes | Makes: 2 Servings

½ pound sausage (cut to bite-size pieces)
1 russet potato
2 teaspoon olive oil
¼ cup yellow onion (diced)
¼ teaspoon salt (or to taste)
¼ teaspoon parsley flakes
¼ teaspoon onion powder (or to taste)
1/8 teaspoon black pepper (or to taste)
1/8 teaspoon paprika (or to taste)

Begin by peeling the potatoes and cutting them to about ½ inch cubes. Soak these diced potatoes in cold water so that the extra starch is removed from the surface. Then drain these potatoes and shift them to a large mixing bowl. Add the olive oil to the bowl and the rest of the seasoning. Once everything is coated throughout, add the sausage and give it one more mix. Rip a large sheet of foil and put the sausages and potatoes inside of it, cooking them for 18 minutes at around 204°C (400°F) in the air fryer, or until the potatoes become fork tender.

Calories 516 Total Fat 37g Saturated Fat 11g Cholesterol 95mg Sodium 1153mg Total Carbohydrate 20.3g Dietary Fibre 2.4g Total Sugars 1.7g Protein 24.5g

Air Fried Avocado Toast

Prep: 15 Minutes | Cook Time: 5 Minutes | Makes: 2 Servings

1 ripe Avocado
2 bread slices
1 teaspoon garlic (minced)
Salt and pepper (to taste)
1 teaspoon lemon juice
Tomatoes (diced, optional)

Take a small bowl and mash the avocados in it, then add the garlic, salt, pepper, and lemon juice, giving everything a good mix. Line the bottom of the air fryer with the bread and spread the avocado mixture on it. Set the temperature of the air fryer to about 204°C (400°F) and cook it for 3 to 5 minutes.
Once done, serve it on the serving plate with a garnish of diced tomatoes.

Calories 243 Total Fat 20.1g Saturated Fat 4.2g Cholesterol 0mg Sodium 71mg Total Carbohydrate 16.1g Dietary Fibre 7.7g Total Sugars 2.6g Protein 3.3g

Blueberry Banana Muffins

Prep: 15 Minutes | Cook Time: 15 Minutes | Makes: 2 Servings

¼ cup sugar
1 egg (lightly whisked)
¼ cup butter (melted)
1 cup whole wheat flour
1 teaspoon baking soda
1 teaspoon baking powder
¼ teaspoon salt
2 bananas (mashed)
1 cup blueberries

Begin by lining the muffin cups with some muffin liners. Take a large mixing bowl and add the cream sugar, eggs, and butter, giving everything a good mix. Once they are mixed, add the remaining dry ingredients and mix them until the batter is nice and smooth. Finally, add in the mashed bananas and blueberries. Take A scoop of the batter and fill the muffin cups with it filling about ¾ of the cup, and put it inside the air fryer cooking it for around 15 minutes at 150°C (300°F).

Calories 705 Total Fat 26.5g Saturated Fat 15.5g Cholesterol 143mg Sodium 1119mg Total Carbohydrate 111.5g Dietary Fiber 6.6g Total Sugars 47g Protein 11.3g

Greek Almond Cookies

Prep: 15 Minutes | Cook Time: 15 Minutes | Makes: 4Servings

3 cups almond flour
¾ cup granulated sugar
1 tablespoon orange zest
¼ teaspoon salt
3 egg whites (slightly beaten)
1 cup almonds (sliced)

Begin by preheating the air fryer to about 177°C (350°F) and lining the bottom of a baking tray with parchment paper. Mix the sugar, orange zest, almond flour, and salt in a large mixing bowl, giving them a good mix. Once the dry ingredients have been mixed, add in the egg whites and mix everything until the dough is wet and is like a paste. Take spoonfuls of the dough, and roll each one in some sliced almonds. Put these cookies on the oiled basket, and flatten them out using a spoon. Bake the cookies for about 15 minutes or until they turn golden brown.

Calories 796 Total Fat 51.8g Saturated Fat 3.9g Cholesterol 0mg
Sodium 203mg Total Carbohydrate 61.2g Dietary Fibre 12.1g
Total Sugars 38.7g Protein 25.7g

Greek Easter Cookies

Prep: 15 Minutes | Cook Time: 22 Minutes | Makes: 4 Servings

1 cup butter
1 cup caster sugar
1 teaspoon vanilla essence
1 tablespoon lemon rind
1 tablespoon orange rind
3 egg yolks
¼ cup milk
2 cups flour
¾ cup self-rising flour
1 egg yolk
Icing sugar

Begin by preheating the air fryer to around 145°C (290°F). Mix the butter and the sugar until they become creamy and then add 1 teaspoon vanilla essence and 1 tablespoon orange and lemon rind. Beat up 3 egg yolks in the same bowl. In another mixing bowl, add the milk, plain flour, and self-raising flour. Mix everything and shift them to the other wet ingredients. Mix everything up and shift it to a flat, floured surface. Take 1 tablespoon of the mixture and make long logs out of it, folding them in half and giving them two twists.

Put these on a baking tray with parchment paper on the bottom. Whisk one egg yolk and water, brushing it over the biscuits, bake them for about 22 minutes or until they turn golden brown.

Calories 827 Total Fat 44.9g Saturated Fat 27.2g Cholesterol 266mg
Sodium 303mg Total Carbohydrate 99.8g Dietary Fibre 1.9g
Total Sugars 51.2g Protein 9.5g

Roasted Nuts Recipe (GF) (DF)

Prep: 15 Minutes | Cook Time: 20 Minutes | Makes: 4 Servings

1 cup almonds
1 cup cashews
1 cup peanuts

Start by heating the air fryer to 160°C (325°F). Add in all the nuts and cook them for about 20 minutes, making sure to toss them halfway so they brown evenly. When done, set them aside and let them cool before storing or eating.

Calories 541 Total Fat 45.7g Saturated Fat 6.5g Cholesterol 0mg
Sodium 12mg Total Carbohydrate 22.2g Dietary Fibre 7.1g
Total Sugars 4.2g   Protein 19.7g

Rosemary Chicken Thighs (GF)

Prep: 12 Minutes | Cook Time: 18 Minutes | Makes: 3 Servings

1.5 pounds chicken thighs
¼ cup olive oil
salt and black pepper, to taste
¼ teaspoon of chopped rosemary
1 teaspoon of lemon juice
¼ teaspoon of lemon zest
1/3 cup of Greek yogurt

In a bowl, combine all the listed ingredients and coat the chicken well with it. Preheat the air fryer to 400 degrees F for a few minutes. Layer parchment paper onto the basket of the air fryer. Cook the chicken for about 18 minutes, flipping halfway through once cooked, serve.

Calories 593 Total Fat 34.1g Saturated Fat 7.4g Cholesterol 203mg
Sodium 203mg Total Carbohydrate 1.1g Dietary Fiber 0.1g
Total Sugars 1g   Protein 67.9g

Chicken Meatballs In Marinara Sauce

Prep: 12 Minutes | Cook Time: 25 Minutes | Makes: 2 Servings

1 /4 cup of onions, minced
1 teaspoon of ginger and garlic paste
1/3 cup bread crumbs
Salt and black pepper, to taste
1 pound chicken, minced
oil spray, for greasing
2 cups marinara sauce

Take a large bowl and mix chicken, breadcrumb, onion, and garlic ginger paste. Combine onions, egg yolks, garlic, crumbs, salt, and pepper in a bowl and mix well. Add the chicken to the bowl.
Make meatballs with your hands. Mist the meatballs with oil spray. Now preheat the air fryer to 204°C (400°F). Add the meatballs to the air fryer and then cook for 20 minutes at 204°C (400°F) Meanwhile, in a skillet add the marinara sauce and then it until warm. Add in the cooked chicken meatballs. Then simmer for 5 minutes and serve and enjoy.

Calories 593 Total Fat 34.1g Saturated Fat 7.4g Cholesterol 203mg
Sodium 203mg Total Carbohydrate 1.1g Dietary Fiber 0.1g
Total Sugars 1g   Protein 67.9g

Roasted Bacon Brussels Sprouts

Prep: 12 Minutes | Cook Time: 20 Minutes | Makes: 2 Servings

1 pound Brussels sprouts
1/3 cup of bacon bits
1 tablespoon Olive Oil
Salt and pepper, to taste

Trim the Brussels sprout bottoms. Then add in the olive oil, salt, and black pepper. Add it to the air fryer Cook for 20 minutes at 400 degrees F. Once the Brussels sprouts are done, add the bacon and toss well with a sprinkle of salt and pepper, then serve it.

Calories 175 Total Fat 9.1g Saturated Fat 1.7g Cholesterol 3mg Sodium 130mg Total Carbohydrate 20.7g Dietary Fibre 8.5g Total Sugars 4.9g Protein 8.9g

Cheesy Zucchini

Prep: 12 Minutes | Cook Time: 25 Minutes | Makes: 2 Servings

1 cup quinoa, rinsed
2 cloves of garlic, minced
2 medium zucchini, cut lengthwise and center core
1 cup red beans, cooked
½ cup almonds, chopped
2 cloves of garlic, chopped
4 tablespoons olive oil
¼ cup Parmesan cheese, for topping

Preheat the air fryer to 400 degrees F for 3 minutes. Meanwhile, heat oil in a skillet and sauté garlic for 1 minute, then add the cooked quinoa and cooked red beans. Cook for 5 minutes. Add the mixture to the cavity for zucchinis and top it off with cheese and almonds. Cook it in the air fryer for 15 minutes at 400 degrees F Once done, serve and enjoy.

Calories 1048 Total Fat 47.1g Saturated Fat 6.2g Cholesterol 3mg Sodium 68mg Total Carbohydrate 123.8g Dietary Fiber 25.1g Total Sugars 6.4g   Protein 41.4g

Wrapped Avocados

Prep: 12 Minutes | Cook Time: 15 Minutes | Makes: 2 Servings

1 medium ripe avocados
6 bacon strips

Ingredient for sauce
1 cup mayonnaise
2 tablespoons Sriracha chili sauce
1 teaspoon grated lime zest

the first step is to preheat the air fryer t0 400 degrees F. Cut the avocados lengthwise and wrap each slice with a bacon strip Place these wrapped wedges in a single layer on a tray in an air-fryer basket. Cook it for 15 minutes. Meanwhile, mix r mayonnaise, Sriracha sauce, and zest. Serve the sauce with wedges.

Calories 505 Total Fat 46.6g Saturated Fat 13.1g Cholesterol 0mg Sodium 914mg Total Carbohydrate 8.8g Dietary Fibre 6.8g Total Sugars 0.5g Protein 13.9g

Air Fryer Cookies

Prep: 12 Minutes | Cook Time: 18 Minutes | Makes: 2 Servings

1 cup quinoa, rinsed
2 cloves of garlic, minced
2 medium zucchini, cut lengthwise and center core
1 cup red beans, cooked
½ cup almonds, chopped
2 cloves of garlic, chopped
4 tablespoons olive oil
¼ cup Parmesan cheese, for topping

Preheat the air fryer to 400 degrees F. Take a small bowl and mix dry ingredients. Set it aside. In a larger bowl, whisk eggs and mix in wet ingredients. Combine both the ingredients. Now take a basket of air fryers and line it with parchment paper. Scoop the cookie dough onto the basket. Place in the air fryer basket and cook for 18 minutes. Once it's done, serve after cooling down.

Calories 1242 Total Fat 92.5g Saturated Fat 56.4g Cholesterol 186mg Sodium 546mg Total Carbohydrate 88.7g Dietary Fiber 4.8g Total Sugars 41.8g Protein 13.8g

Figs With Honey And Mascarpone

Prep: 12 Minutes | Cook Time: 10 Minutes | Makes: 5 Servings

10 figs
1/3 cup coconut oil
2 tablespoons maple syrup
1/2 cup mascarpone
1 teaspoon of walnuts
1 teaspoon of Rose water, as needed

Preheat the air fryer to 204°C (400°F). Cut the top of all the figs and squeeze it open. Place it inside the air fryer basket. Drizzle coconut oil on top along with maple syrup. Sprinkle rose water and cook in an air fryer for 8 minutes, serve it with a dollop of mascarpone and top it off with walnuts. Enjoy.

Calories 299 Total Fat 19.3g Saturated Fat 15.3g Cholesterol 16mg Sodium 31mg Total Carbohydrate 30.7g Dietary Fibre 3.8g Total Sugars 23.1g Protein 4.9g

Simple Breakfast Recipe

Prep: 12 Minutes | Cook Time: 12 Minutes | Makes: 2 Servings

1 1/2 cups whole wheat flour
1 teaspoon baking powder
Pinch of salt
4 tablespoons brown sugar
1/3 cup milk

Mix all the ingredients in a bowl and add milk. Make small shapes with hands Coat the shapes with oil.
Place in the air fryer, and cook it for 12 minutes.
Serve once puffed.
Enjoy.

Calories 432 Total Fat 1.8g Saturated Fat 0.7g Cholesterol 3mg Sodium 106mg Total Carbohydrate 92.4g Dietary Fiber 2.6g Total Sugars 19.5g Protein 11g

Pancakes with Raspberry Topping

Prep: 12 Minutes | Cook Time: 18 Minutes | Makes: 2 Servings

2 tablespoons coconut oil, melted
4 organic eggs
½ cup whole wheat flour
½ cup almond milk
2 teaspoons vanilla
2 cups fresh raspberry
2 tablespoons of Maple syrup, drizzle

Preheat the air fryer to 204°C (400°F). Take a small pan that adjusts in an air fryer basket. Take a bowl and combine oil, eggs, flour, almond milk, and vanilla. Coat the pan with the oil spray pour package batter into the pan. Top with raspberries. Cook for 16-18 minutes, once done, serve.

Calories 609 Total Fat 37g Saturated Fat 27.2g Cholesterol 327mg Sodium 135mg Total Carbohydrate 58.8g Dietary Fibre 10.2g Total Sugars 27.2g Protein 16.7g

Air-Fryer Lime Macaroons

Prep: 12 Minutes | Cook Time: 10 Minutes | Makes: 2 Servings

1 cup almond butter, softened
3/4 cup sugar
2 large eggs, room temperature
1 teaspoon vanilla extract
2.5 cups quick-cooking oats
1.5 cups whole wheat flour
1 teaspoon vanilla extract
1 teaspoon baking powder
salt, pinch
2 cups semisweet chocolate chips
1 cup chopped walnuts

Preheat the air fryer to 204°C (400°F). Take a large bowl and add eggs, butter, sugar, and whisk for 5 minutes. Then add vanilla, baking powder, salt, chocolate chips, nuts, oats, and wholewheat flour. Mix and drip dough onto parchment line basket. Cook for 10 minutes. Once done, serve

Calories 2645 Total Fat 118g Saturated Fat 45.3g Cholesterol 186mg Sodium 160mg Total Carbohydrate 369.4g Dietary Fibre 30g 107% Total Sugars 189.9g Protein 46.2g

Date And Walnut Bread

Prep: 12 Minutes | Cook Time: 18 Minutes | Makes: 4 Servings

2.5 cup chopped dates
1/2 cup butter
1 cup hot water
1/4 cup brown sugar
2 eggs
1.5 cup whole wheat flour
¼ teaspoon baking soda
¼ teaspoon baking powder
salt, pinch
1/3 cup diced walnuts

Take a pan and pour hot water in it. Add the dates and then remove the pits and peel. Add butter and mix well Then add a little bit of warm water. Take a bowl and combine flour, brown sugar, egg, baking soda, baking powder, and salt. Mix it very well. Grease an air fryer with oil. Add the walnuts and mix to the flour mixture and mix well to form a dough. Pour the batter into the loaf pan. Cook for 12-18 minutes at 204°C (400°F) in the air fryer. Serve once cool.

Calories 818 Total Fat 32.3g Saturated Fat 15.7g Cholesterol 143mg Sodium 320mg Total Carbohydrate 129.5g Dietary Fibre 10.9g Total Sugars 79.7g Protein 13.1g

Date Cookies

Prep: 12 Minutes | Cook Time: 11 Minutes | Makes: 4 Servings

2 cups chopped dates
½ cup chopped pecans
½ cup water
1very ripe banana, mashed
2large egg, lightly beaten
4 tablespoons almond butter, melted
1 teaspoon vanilla extract
2cups wheat flour
2teaspoon baking powder
2teaspoon cinnamon
pinch of salt

Preheat the air fryer to 400 degrees F. Line a baking sheet with parchment paper. Mix the pecans, dates, pecans, water, banana, egg, butter, and vanilla extract in a large bowl. Whisk the remaining ingredient in a large bowl. Now combine both the bowl ingredients. Drop dough onto the prepared baking sheet. Bake it in the preheated air fryer. Cook for 11 minutes. Transfer it to rack to cool then serve.

Calories 656 Total Fat 14.5g Saturated Fat 2.2g Cholesterol 93mg Sodium 82mg Total Carbohydrate 123.6g Dietary Fiber 11.3g Total Sugars 60.7g Protein 15.4g

Chocolate Vanilla Cupcake

Prep: 14 Minutes | Cook Time: 15 Minutes | Makes: 2 Servings

1 cup sugar
1 cup peanut butter
4 eggs
1/2 cup almond milk
1 3/4 whole wheat flour
1/4 tablespoon Vanilla extract

Combine sugar, butter, eggs, almond milk, whole wheat flour, and vanilla extract. Spoon this batter into the ramekins. Cook it in the air fryer for 400 degrees F, for 15 minutes. Then serve and enjoy.

Calories 1672 Total Fat 79.4g Saturated Fat 27.3g Cholesterol 327mg Sodium 640mg Total Carbohydrate 206g Dietary Fiber 10.7g Total Sugars 113.5g Protein 50.8g

Air Fryer Peanut Butter Cookies

Prep: 12 Minutes | Cook Time: 8 Minutes | Makes:2 Servings

1 Cup Peanut Butter
1 cup brown Sugar
1 large Egg

Mix all of the ingredients in a bowl.
Spray air fryer basket with oil spray.
Preheat the air fryer to 204°C (400°F).
Place rounded balls of dough onto the basket, and cook for 8 minutes.
Serve once cool.

Calories 1069 Total Fat 67.4g Saturated Fat 14.5g Cholesterol 93mg Sodium 648mg Total Carbohydrate 96.7g Dietary Fibre 7.7g Total Sugars 82.6g Protein 35.5g

Apples With Cinnamon

Prep: 12 Minutes | Cook Time: 15 Minutes | Makes: 4 Servings

4 Granny Smith Apples Sliced and Cored
3 tablespoons of corn flour
1 tsp cinnamon
1 tbsp maple syrup
2 tablespoons of coconut shaving
1 cup coconut cream
directions

Peel and then cut the apples into slices. Sprinkle the corn starch, cinnamon, and maple syrup over the entire slice. Add it to your air fryer and cook for 204°C (400°F) for 15 minutes.
Top with coconut shaving and coconut cream! Enjoy!

Calories 270 Total Fat 15.5g 20% Saturated Fat 13.5g Cholesterol 0mg
Sodium 25mg Total Carbohydrate 35.4g Dietary Fibre 7.8g
Total Sugars 23.3g Protein 1.8g

Roasted Oranges (GF)(DF)

Prep: 12 Minutes | Cook Time: 10 Minutes | Makes: 2 Servings

2 medium oranges
2 tablespoons honey
2 teaspoons cinnamon

Slice the oranges in half. Sprinkle the cinnamon on the orange halves. Then drizzle the honey.
Place it in an air fryer and cook for 10 minutes at 182°C (360°F). Once cooked, serve.

Calories 131 Total Fat 0.2g Saturated Fat 0g Cholesterol 0mg
Sodium 1mg Total Carbohydrate 34.5g Dietary Fibre 4.4g
Total Sugars 29.6g Protein 1.4g

Caramelized Stone Fruit (GF)

Prep: 12 Minutes | Cook Time: 12 Minutes | Makes: 2 Servings

1 pound of peaches, sliced
1 cup plums, sliced
2 apricots, sliced
1 tablespoon Maple syrup
1/2 tablespoon Coconut flakes
1/4 tsp Cinnamon, optional
pinch of salt, optional

Line a basket with parchment papers. Brush the fruit slices with maple syrup and coat with coconut flakes. Sprinkle salt and cinnamon. Cook it in the air fryer for 177°C (350°F) for 12 minutes, flipping halfway through.
Then serve.

Calories 92 Total Fat 1g Saturated Fat 0.4g Cholesterol 0mg
Sodium 79mg Total Carbohydrate 22g Dietary Fibre 2.5g
Total Sugars 19.7g Protein 1.5g

Mini Peach & Thyme Cobblers (GF) (DF)

Prep: 12 Minutes | Cook Time: 25 Minutes | Makes: 4 Servings

2 large peaches, peeled, pitted, and sliced into halves
2 tablespoons peanut butter
23 tablespoons wholewheat flour
3 Tablespoons brown sugar
4 Tablespoons pecans (or walnuts), finely chopped
2 sprigs fresh thyme, chopped

Place peach halves sided up in Air Fryer basket. Cook for 20 minutes t 204°C (400°F), flipping halfway through. Meanwhile, prepare the cobbler by taking a medium-sized bowl and combining brown sugar, wheat flour, and pecans. When peaches are ready remove them from the air fryer basket and cut them into bite-size pieces. Fill each ramekin with butter mix then thyme and top with peach pieces. Cook for 5 minutes in an air fryer, then serve.

Calories 369 Total Fat 14.8g Saturated Fat 2g Cholesterol 0mg Sodium 41mg Total Carbohydrate 52.9g Dietary Fibre 5.1g Total Sugars 15g   Protein 9.1g

Fruit Roll-Ups (GF)

Prep: 15 Minutes | Cook Time: 8 hours | Makes: 4 Servings

2 cups fresh strawberries
3 tbsp Splenda
1/2 lemon, juiced

Take a high-speed blender and pulse together strawberries, sugar, and lemon juice. Take a dehydrating rack lined with parchment paper. Spread the mixture across the paper on the dehydrator rack. Press the dehydrate button of the air fryer oven at 60°C (140°F). Dehydrate for 8 hours. It will be no longer be sticky at the end. Slice and serve.

Calories 70 Total Fat 0.2g Saturated Fat 0g Cholesterol 0mg Sodium 1mg Total Carbohydrate 15.2g Dietary Fibre 1.6g Total Sugars 12.7g   Protein 0.6g

Vanilla Bean Chia Pudding (GF) (DF)

Prep: 12 Minutes | Cook Time: 13 Minutes | Makes: 1 Serving

2 ounces semolina
2 cups coconut milk
1 teaspoon vanilla extract

Take a mixing bowl, add whisk all of the ingredients together.
Pour it into a small heat-proof pan.
Let it cook in the air fryer at 150°C (300°F) for 13 minutes.
Wait five minutes and whisk it well.
Add it to the refrigerator and serve once cool and solid in texture
Cover and refrigerate until set, or add to individual jars, ready for lunchboxes before adding to the fridge or freezer.

Calories 1320 Total Fat 115g Saturated Fat 101.6g Cholesterol 0mg Sodium 73mg Total Carbohydrate 68.4g Dietary Fibre 12.8g 4 Total Sugars 16.6g   Protein 18.2g

Blueberries Bread Pudding

Prep: 12 Minutes | Cook Time: 25 Minutes | Makes: 2 Servings

7 eggs, organic
1/3 cup heavy cream
2 teaspoons orange liqueur
Salt, to taste
4 whole-wheat buns
1/4 cup blueberries

Whisk eggs in a bowl and add cream and sugar. Mix until sugar dissolves. Then add the orange liqueur, blueberries, and salt. Put the bun pieces on a plate, then dip in the egg mixture. Coat the bun pieces with the egg mixture. And add it to a heat-proof bowl. Cook for 25 minutes at 204°C (400°F) inside air fryer basket. Serve and enjoy once everything is ready.

Calories 1099 Total Fat 38.8g Saturated Fat 12.4g Cholesterol 600mg Sodium 3281mg Total Carbohydrate 102.4g Dietary Fibre 22.4g Total Sugars 25g Protein 63.9g

Coated Shrimp (DF)

Prep: 15 Minutes | Cook Time: 6 Minutes| Makes: 1 Serving

6 ounces shrimp
sale and black pepper
1 cup Panko bread crumbs
1 cup coconut milk

Preheat the air fryer to 204°C (400°F). Mix coconut milk with salt and pepper. Dip shrimp in coconut milk then coat with Panko breadcrumbs. Cook in the air fryer for 6 minutes, shaking halfway through. Serve it, once done.

Calories 1181 Total Fat 65.8g Saturated Fat 52.9g Cholesterol 358mg Sodium 1242mg Total Carbohydrate 93.6g Dietary Fibre 10.1g Total Sugars 14.7g Protein 58.7g

Air Fryer Spicy Wings (GF)

Prep: 12 Minutes | Cook Time: 22 Minutes | Makes: 2 Servings

2 pounds chicken wings
1 teaspoon Mediterranean style Oregano
2 teaspoons of olive oil
4 cloves of garlic
1 teaspoon thyme
salt and black pepper, to taste
¼ teaspoon Cayenne pepper
2 tablespoons Lemon juice

Preheat the air fryer to 204°C (400°F). Mix oil, garlic, thyme, black pepper, salt, cayenne pepper, lemon juice in a bowl and coat the wings with it. Place the chicken in an air fryer basket lined with parchment paper. Cook for 22 minutes at 204°C (400°F), flipping halfway through. Allow for 5 minutes of rest before baking the next batch.

Calories 919 Total Fat 38.6g Saturated Fat 10.1g Cholesterol 404mg Sodium 395mg Total Carbohydrate 3.3g Dietary Fibre 0.8g Total Sugars 0.4g Protein 131.9g

Chicken Cheese Balls (GF)

Prep: 12 Minutes | Cook Time: 12 Minutes | Makes: 2 Servings

1 rotisserie chicken
1/3 cup hot sauce
1 cup Sharp Cheddar Shreds
1 teaspoon ground black pepper
1 cup almond flour
4 eggs
1 cup Panko bread crumbs

Take a blender and pulse the chicken along with pepper, cheese, and hot sauce. Make small balls out of the chicken mixture. In a large bowl mix the flour and breadcrumbs. Whisk the egg in a shallow bowl. Roll each ball in flour, then the egg, and then roll in the breadcrumbs. Cook inside of the air fryer for 18 mites at 177°C (350°F). Serve hot.

Calories 982 Total Fat 56.9g Saturated Fat 17.4g Cholesterol 440mg Sodium 2154mg Total Carbohydrate 58.4g Dietary Fibre 8.8g Total Sugars 4.5g Protein 62.1g

Air Fryer Cheese Crackers

Prep: 15 Minutes | Cook Time: 5 Minutes| Makes: 1 Serving

1 package ultra-thin cheese, personal choice

Place thin cheese slices in an air fryer basket lined with parchment paper. Cook it in the Air fryer at 400 degrees Fahrenheit for 5 minutes. Once done, serve.

Calories 100 Total Fat 3g Saturated Fat 1g Cholesterol 0mg Sodium 250mg Total Carbohydrate 15g Dietary Fiber 1g Total Sugars 0g Protein 2g

Air Fryer Honey Goat Cheese Balls

Prep: 15 Minutes | Cook Time: 12 Minutes| Makes: 2 Servings

12 ounces soft goat cheese
2 large eggs, beaten
1 cup Panko bread crumbs
oil spray, for greasing

Divide the goat cheese into 24 pieces and roll them in round balls. Then put it in the freezer for 30 minutes. Remove the frozen goat cheese balls from the freezer and coat them with, beaten egg, and then breadcrumbs. Once all are coated, freezer for up to 12 hours. Once decided to cook arrange them in an air fryer basket. Lightly spray with oil. Cook for 12 minutes at 204°C (400°F), or until golden brown.

Calories 919 Total Fat 38.6g Saturated Fat 10.1g Cholesterol 404mg Sodium 395mg Total Carbohydrate 3.3g Dietary Fibre 0.8g Total Sugars 0.4g Protein 131.9g

Blueberry Pie

Prep: 12 Minutes | Cook Time: 12 Minutes | Makes: 2 Servings

1 box Store-Bought Pie Dough, whole wheat
1 cup blueberries, cubed
4 tablespoons of coconut cream
2 tablespoons of almonds
1 egg white, for brushing

Lay the rolled out pastry dough in a round pie dish, and trim excess from edges. Brush it with egg white around the edge. Fill it with blueberries, almonds, and coconut cream. Add a round pastry lid. Press the edges and use a fork to seal the edges. Cook at 204°C (400°F) for 10 -12 minutes inside air fryer.
Once done, serve.

Calories 378 Total Fat 22.9g Saturated Fat 12.6g Cholesterol 5mg Sodium 182mg Total Carbohydrate 40.1g Dietary Fibre 3.6g 13% Total Sugars 28.1g Protein 6.8g

Baked Mangoes

Prep: 12 Minutes | Cook Time: 16 Minutes | Makes: 2 Servings

4 puff pastry sheets, whole wheat
2 1/4 cups mango custard, cooked
2 mangos, peeled
coconut cream, as needed for topping

Peel and chop the mangos. Put the mango custard into the middle of the pastry sheets. Then top it with mango pieces and mango custard. Close the pastry to form parcels. Seal the edges. Cook at 177°C (350°F) for 16 minutes in an air fryer basket. Serve with coconut cream

Calories 1037 Total Fat 46.4g Saturated Fat 16g Cholesterol 50mg Sodium 314mg Total Carbohydrate 150.6g Dietary Fibre 7g 25% Total Sugars 99.4g Protein 9.8g

Orange Cornmeal Cake

Prep: 10 Minutes | Cook Time: 22 Minutes | Makes: 2 Servings

2 cups all-purpose flour
1 cup yellow cornmeal
1cup white sugar
1 teaspoon baking soda
1/2 cup olive oil
1 cup orange juice, divided
1 teaspoon vanilla
½ cup powdered sugar
oil spray, for greasing

Grease the baking pan with oil spray and set it aside. In a bowl add all the listed ingredients and mix well. Then pour it into a baking pan. Bake it in the air fryer and bake for 22 minutes at 177°C (350°F). Remove the cake from the air fryer and let it cool.
Slice and serve.

Calories 1664 Total Fat 54.4g Saturated Fat 7.8g Cholesterol 0mg Sodium 655mg Total Carbohydrate 285.3g Dietary Fibre 8.1g Total Sugars 140.8g Protein 18.7g

Blueberry Muffins

Prep: 12 Minutes | Cook Time: 18 Minutes | Makes: 2 Servings

3 eggs
1/4 cup sugar
¼ cup melted butter
4 tablespoons of almond milk
1/2 teaspoon of lemon zest
1 /2 teaspoon of vanilla extract
1 teaspoon of baking powder
1.5 cups whole wheat flour
1/4 cup oats
1 cup blueberries

Coat a few ramekins with oil spray. Combine the eggs, butter, milk, lemon zest, and vanilla essence until mixed well in a bowl. Then add the remaining ingredients one by one. Mix into a batter and pour it in ramekins at the end top with blueberries. Do not fill ramekins to the top. Cook for 18 minutes at 204°C (400°F) inside air fryer. Serve the muffins for breakfast after they're done.

Calories 888 Total Fat 38.6g Saturated Fat 23.2g Cholesterol 307mg Sodium 343mg Total Carbohydrate 117.6g Dietary Fibre 6.1g Total Sugars 34.2g Protein 20.8g

Chocolate Pudding

Prep: 12 Minutes | Cook Time: 5 Minutes | Makes: 2 Servings

4 tablespoons cocoa powder
10 ounces Greek yogurt
½ teaspoon of mint extract
4 tablespoons of sugar
1 cup almond flour

Grease the ramekins with oil spray. Mix almond flour, cocoa powder, sugar, with mint extract and microwave for 2 minutes. Then layer it onto the bottom of the ramekins. Whisk the yogurt and top it off the ramekins. Add it to the air fryer basket and cook to 177°C (350°F), for 5 minutes. Once it's done, serve.

Calories 423 Total Fat 13.1g Saturated Fat 3.8g Cholesterol 7mg Sodium 56mg Total Carbohydrate 58.1g Dietary Fibre 10.2g 36% Total Sugars 6.3g Protein 24.6g

Chocolate Brownies (GF)

Prep: 12 Minutes | Cook Time: 12 Minutes | Makes: 2 Servings

1 cup Almond Flour
4 tablespoons Stevia
1/3 teaspoon Baking Powder
4 tablespoons of cocoa powder
4 Egg
6 tablespoons butter, melted
4 tablespoons Chocolate chip
10 walnuts, crushed

Preheat the air fryer to 204°C (400°F). Whisk together the almond flour, stevia, baking powder, cocoa powder, and stevia. Whisk the egg and melted butter and add it to the dry ingredients to beat it well. Stir in the walnuts and chocolate chips. Pour this to oil-greased ramekins. Cook the cakes for 12 minutes at 204°C (400°F).

Calories 1145 Total Fat 100.6g Saturated Fat 33.1g Cholesterol 424mg Sodium 409mg Total Carbohydrate 35.4g Dietary Fibre 12.6g Total Sugars 12.2g Protein 36.4g

Crab Sticks

Prep: 12 Minutes | Cook Time: 5 Minutes | Makes: 2 Servings

220 grams imitation crab sticks
Cooking spray

unroll the crab sticks with care and unpeel it, then cut them into strips. Preheat the air fryer for 5 minutes at 204°C (400°F).
add the crab sticks to the oiled basket of the air fryer and cook for 5 minutes. Pull the basket out of the air fryer.
Serve with garlic butter.

Calories 109 Total Fat 1g Saturated Fat 0g Cholesterol 23mg Sodium 840mg Total Carbohydrate 13.8g Dietary Fibre 0g Total Sugars 4.6g Protein 10.7g

Old Bay Seasoned Crab Leg (GF) (DF)

Prep: 13 Minutes | Cook Time: 5 Minutes | Makes: 1 Serving

1 Pound crab legs cleaned and scrubbed
2 tablespoons olive oil
1 teaspoon old bay seasoning
½ teaspoon garlic powder

Coat the crab legs with olive oil, old bay, and garlic powder.
Place the legs in foil paper. Cook in the air fryer at 380 degrees F for 5 minutes. Remove from the air fryer and foil paper.
serve hot.

Calories 717 Total Fat 34.9g Saturated Fat 4g Cholesterol 252mg Sodium 5498mg Total Carbohydrate 4.1g Dietary Fiber 0.6g Total Sugars 1.4g Protein 88g

Fish Balls

Prep: 13 Minutes | Cook Time: 12 Minutes | Makes: 2 Servings

16 ounces salmon, minced
6 tablespoons of breadcrumbs
Salt and pepper, to taste
2eggs

Coat the basket of your air fryer with nonstick spray.
Combine all of the ingredients in a bowl.
Make a few golf ball-sized balls out of your mixture.
Put the crab cake balls in the air fryer and cook for 12 minutes at 375 degrees, or until golden and crispy.

Calories 443 Total Fat 19.4g Saturated Fat 3.6g Cholesterol 264mg Sodium 310mg Total Carbohydrate 15g Dietary Fiber 0.9g Total Sugars 1.6g Protein 52.3g

Parmesan Sriracha Cauliflower

Prep: 12 Minutes | Cook Time: 20 Minutes | Makes: 2 Servings

1 cup cauliflowers cut smaller
1 teaspoon Sriracha sauce
2 teaspoons olive oil
1/3 cup of parmesan, hard

Add the florets, Sriracha, and oil to a bowl and toss well
Transfer it to an air fryer basket lined with parchment paper.
Cook for 20 minutes at 230°C (450°F).
Serve with a sprinkle of Parmesan cheese once done.

Calories 68 Total Fat 5.7g Saturated Fat 1.4g Cholesterol 3mg
Sodium 66mg Total Carbohydrate 2.8g Dietary Fibre 1.3g
Total Sugars 1.2g Protein 2.5g

Garlic Bread

Prep: 10 Minutes | Cook Time: 10 Minutes | Makes: 2 Servings

1 tablespoon butter
2 teaspoons chopped parsley
2 cloves garlic, chopped fine
½ cup grated Parmesan cheese
1 large loaf of whole wheat bread

Preheat the air fryer to 204°C (400°F) for a few minutes. Combine and mix butter, parsley, garlic cloves, and Parmesan cheese. Spread it over bread slices. Arrange the slices to the air fryer basket and cook for 10 minutes at 204°C (400°F). Once done, serve

Calories 123 Total Fat 7.8g Saturated Fat 4.7g Cholesterol 20mg
Sodium 197mg Total Carbohydrate 9.3g Dietary Fibre 1.6g
Total Sugars 1g Protein 4.5g

Bacon-Wrapped Shrimp With Pitta

Prep: 12 Minutes | Cook Time: 8 Minutes | Makes: 2 Servings

20 jumbo raw shrimp, no shell
10 slices bacon, sliced in half
8 Tablespoons cream cheese
thin slices of jalapeno
bbq sauce

Butterfly cut shrimps, and add jalapenos sliced into the opening, along with cream cheese. Take half slice of bacon and wrap the shrimp with it. Refrigerate for 60 minutes Place the pitta on the bottom of the air fryer Put shrimp on top. Cook for 8 minutes at 177°C (350°F). Serve it up with bbq sauce.

Calories 1854 Total Fat 73.6g Saturated Fat 21.8g Cholesterol 1848mg
Sodium 4013mg Total Carbohydrate 2.4g Dietary Fibre 0g
Total Sugars 0.1g Protein 268.2g

Mint Lamb With Toasted Hazelnuts And Peas

Prep: 12 Minutes | Cook Time: 25 Minutes | Makes: 2 Servings

1/2 cup hazelnuts
1,4 pounds of shoulder of lamb cut into 2 inches x 1 inch strips
2 tablespoons hazelnut oil
2 tablespoons fresh mint leaves chopped
1 cup peas
Olive oil spray, for greasing
2 tablespoons white wine
Salt and black pepper, to taste

Roast the hazelnuts on a skillet then set aside in a bowl mix oil, salt, and pepper. Then add lamb and coat well. Put the mint leaves with the seasoned lamb in air fryer basket, and grease with oil spray. Then scatter the toasted hazelnuts and wine on top of the lamb. Add peas on top. Spray all ingredients with oil. Cook for 25 minutes at 204°C (400°F). Serve with juice drizzled on top.

Calories 1030 Total Fat 67g Saturated Fat 16.3g Cholesterol 283mg Sodium 225mg Total Carbohydrate 15.1g Dietary Fibre 6.1g Total Sugars 5.3g Protein 87.7g

Steak Fajitas With Onions And Peppers

Prep: 12 Minutes | Cook Time: 13-15 Minutes | Makes: 2 Servings

1 pound Thin Cut Steak
Black pepper, to taste
Salt, to taste
1/2 Cup White Onions Sliced
1 Packet Gluten Free Fajita Seasoning
Olive Oil Spray
Gluten-Free Corn Tortillas or Flour Tortillas

Layer the basket of the air fryer with foil and coat it with the spray. Slice the steak into about ¼ inch slices. Coat the steak with salt, peppers, fajita seasoning, and top with onions. Add to the air fryer basket. Cook for 8 minutes at 200°C (390°F), flipping halfway. Continue cooking for an additional 5 minutes, until the desired doneness.
Serve by topping on to wholewheat tortillas.

Calories 537 Total Fat 33.4g Saturated Fat 9.5g Cholesterol 133mg Sodium 1405mg Total Carbohydrate 7.4g Dietary Fibre 0.8g Total Sugars 0.1g Protein 47.1g

Greek Mediterranean Loaded Potatoes (GF)

Prep: 12 Minutes | Cook Time: 50 Minutes | Makes: 2 Servings

3 baked potatoes
1 tbsp oil
6 cups spinach
1/2 cup chopped artichoke hearts
2 tbsp chopped sun-dried tomatoes
2 tbsp lemon juice
2 tbsp olive oil
2 chopped clove garlic
1/4 tsp dried oregano
1 cup yogurt
1/2 cup feta cheese
2 tbsp chopped chives

Take a medium bowl and place the oiled potato into it. Cook the potatoes in the air fryer on dual heat level for 50 minutes. Once cooked, keep the potatoes aside to cool down a little. Meanwhile, take a mixing bowl and add spinach, tomatoes, garlic, lemon juice, oregano, and olive oil. Whisk it well. Then place the bowl in the air fryer and cook until the leaves are wilted. Now, take the baked potato and cut it in half and place the spinach mixture on the potato. You can add yogurt, feta cheese, chives as toppings, and serve.

Calories 611 Total Fat 31.2g Saturated Fat 10g Cholesterol 41mg Sodium 644mg Total Carbohydrate 65.3g Dietary Fibre 8.1g Total Sugars 13.4g Protein 22g

Greek Air Fryer Chicken Kabobs

Prep: 22 Minutes | Cook Time: 15 Minutes | Makes: 2 Servings

FOR THE GREEK MARINADE:
½ cup red wine vinegar
1/3 cup olive oil
2 tbsp dried oregano
3 garlic cloves
2 tbsp finely chopped parsley
½ tsp salt
½ tsp pepper

FOR THE CHICKEN KABOBS:
2 pounds chopped chicken breasts
2 sweet chopped bell peppers
1 chopped onion
8 ounces chopped white button mushrooms

Take a medium bowl and prepare the Greek marinade by combing all the ingredients into the bowl. Mix it well. Then add the chicken to the mixture and marinate for 6-8 hours in the refrigerator. Now, arrange the chicken and the veggies in the skewer. Preheat the air fryer to 193°C (380°F) for 15 minutes. Then place the skewered in the air fryer and cook for 15 minutes. Once the chicken is cooked, serve the kabobs with Greek marinade and sprinkle parsley.

Calories 499 Total Fat 35.6g Saturated Fat 5.2g Cholesterol 0mg Sodium 613mg Total Carbohydrate 44.5g Dietary Fibre 13.9g Total Sugars 21.7g Protein 10.2g

Air Fryer Greek Salmon

Prep: 12 Minutes | Cook Time: 10 Minutes | Makes: 2 Servings

For the Salmon

6 salmon fillets
1 tbsp olive oil
1 tbsp lemon juice
2 garlic cloves pressed
½ tsp dried oregano
4 garlic cloves, minced
½ tsp dried dill
¼ tsp red chili pepper flakes
salt and black pepper, to taste

For the Greek Salad:
4 tbsp extra virgin olive oil
3 tbsp red wine vinegar
½ tsp dried oregano
1 tsp salt
1 tsp black pepper
3 vine-ripened tomatoes
1 Peeled cucumbers
1 Chopped onions
4 ounces black kalamata olives
Chopped parsley
2 ounces feta cheese

Clean and pat dry the salmon using a kitchen towel.
Then place the fillets in the small bowl.
Now, add olive oil, lemon juice, dill, oregano, pepper flakes, and garlic to the bowl.
Carefully coat the salmon in the mixture and marinate for 30 minutes.
Brush your air fryer basket with oil spray and place the salmon in the air fryer basket.
Cook the salmon for 10 minutes at 204°C (400°F).
Meanwhile, take another bowl and add all the Greek salad ingredients to it.
Once the salmon is cooked, serve the salmon with the veggies and enjoy.

Calories 913 Total Fat 47.8g Saturated Fat 10.2g Cholesterol 261mg Sodium 1817mg Total Carbohydrate 14.2g Dietary Fiber 2.2g Total Sugars 6.6g Protein 109.3g

Lamb Sandwich

Prep: 12 Minutes | Cook Time: 25 Minutes | Makes: 2 Servings

12 strips of bacon
6 slices of whole Wheat bread
¼ cup ranch dressing
1 pound of cooked lamb meat
4 slice parmesans cheese
2 teaspoons salted butter

Cook the bacon strip in an oil-coated air fryer basket for 10 minutes at 204°C (400°F), flipping halfway through. Take out and set aside. Butter the two bread slices and add them to the air fryer basket. Layer it with the slices with ranch dressing, lamb meat, and at the end the cooked bacon slices top with cheese.
Cook for 10 minutes at 204°C (400°F). Once cheese melts, serve

Calories 856 Total Fat 38.9g Saturated Fat 18.5g Cholesterol 171mg Sodium 2415mg Total Carbohydrate 58.5g Dietary Fibre 10g Total Sugars 11.9g Protein 64.4g

Air Fryer Turkey Cutlets With Mushroom Sauce

Prep: 12 Minutes | Cook Time: 125 Minutes | Makes: 2 Servings

1.5 pounds ground turkey
2 tablespoon olive oil
salt and pepper, to taste

MUSHROOM SAUCE

1 Can cream of mushroom soup
1 cup milk

Take a bowl and turkey, olive oil, salt, pepper.mix it well, and make patties. Preheat your air fryer to 204°C (400°F). Coat the turkey breast cutlets with butter. Put the turkey cutlers in the air fryer and cook for 12minutes, flipping halfway through. Meanwhile, heat the milk, cream of mushroom soup in a cooking pot over medium heat. Until thick. Remove turkey cutlets and serve with the mushroom sauce.

Calories 969 Total Fat 62.4g Saturated Fat 11.7g Cholesterol 357mg Sodium 1364mg Total Carbohydrate 15.8g Dietary Fibre 0g Total Sugars 7.6g Protein 99.4g

Cheesy Salmon Parmesan (GF)

Prep: 12 Minutes | Cook Time: 8 Minutes | Makes: 2 Servings

1.5 pounds ground turkey
2tablespoon olive oil
salt and pepper, to taste

MUSHROOM SAUCE

1 Can cream of mushroom soup
1 cup milk

Season the salmon fillet with cayenne pepper, lemon juice, minced garlic, olive oil salt, and black pepper. Spray the air fryer basket with oil. Put the salmon on tot basket. Air fry at 350°F for 8 minutes. Serve by sprinkling cheese on top, once done.

Calories 443 Total Fat 28.9g Saturated Fat 4.6g Cholesterol 103mg Sodium 136mg 6% Total Carbohydrate 2.4g Dietary Fibre 0.2g Total Sugars 0.3g Protein 45.6g

Classic Salmon (GF)

Prep: 17 Minutes | Cook Time: 8 Minutes | Makes: 2 Servings

1 pound of salmon fillets
salt and ground black pepper to taste
2 tablespoons of extra-virgin olive oil
2 teaspoons of whole grain mustard
1 teaspoon of brown sugar
1 clove garlic, minced
1/2 tsp. thyme leave
oil spray, for coating
cooking spray

Preheat your air fryer to 204°C (400°F). Season the salmon fillets with salt, garlic, thyme, sugar, oil, mustard, and pepper. Coat I the air fryer basket with oil spray. Cook for 8 minutes, in an air fryer. Then serve

Calories 434 Total Fat 28.5g Saturated Fat 4.1g Cholesterol 100mg Sodium 123mg Total Carbohydrate 2.5g Dietary Fibre 0.1g Total Sugars 1.5g Protein 44.1g

Crab Cake Fritters

Prep: 14 Minutes | Cook Time: 12 Minutes | Makes: 2 Servings

12 ounces of crab meat
6 tablespoons of breadcrumbs
Salt and pepper, to taste
2 large organic eggs

Coat the basket of your air fryer with oil spray. Combine all of the ingredients in a bowl and make fritter shapes Coat the shapes with oil from both sides. Put it inside the basket of the air fryer and cook for 12 minutes, flipping halfway through at 177°C (350°F). Once it's golden and crispy, serve enjoy.

Calories 304 Total Fat 9.1g Saturated Fat 1.8g Cholesterol 277mg Sodium 1281mg Total Carbohydrate 18g Dietary Fibre 0.9g Total Sugars 1.7g Protein 30.3g

Sirloin Steak with Sour Cream

Prep: 15 Minutes | Cook Time: 12Minutes | Makes: 2 Servings

1.5 pounds beef sirloin steak, cut into strips
¼ cup olive oil
½ cup diced tomatoes, un-drained
4 ounces green beans, halved
4 ounces of frozen pearl onions, thawed
1 tablespoon paprika
1 cup sour cream
Salt and pepper, to taste

Preheat the air fryer to 204°C (400°F).
Combine the steak bites with paprika, salt, pepper, tomatoes, green beans, onions, paprika, salt, and pepper in a bowl.
Drizzle with oil and mix well.
Drop it into your air fryer basket, and cook for 12 minutes.
Remove the basket from the air fryer and allow the meat to absorb the juices.
Serve with sour cream.

Calories 443 Total Fat 28.9g Saturated Fat 4.6g Cholesterol 103mg Sodium 136mg 6% Total Carbohydrate 2.4g Dietary Fibre 0.2g Total Sugars 0.3g Protein 45.6g

Greek Yogurt And Herbed Chicken Wings (GF)

Prep: 12 Minutes | Cook Time: 1 8Minutes | Makes: 2 Servings

1/2 cup Greek yogurt
1 tablespoon minced garlic
1 /4 teaspoon turmeric
1 /2 tablespoon paprika
1 /2 teaspoon red cayenne pepper
1 /2 teaspoon salt or to taste
1 pound chicken wings
1 cup Red Onions, sliced
1 Lemon Juice
Sumac to finish, optional

Combine Greek yogurt, garlic, turmeric, paprika, red cayenne pepper, salt, pepper, wings, lemon juice, and onion in a bowl.

Mix all the ingredients for fine coating. Then add it to the air fryer basket greased with oil spray. Cook for 204°C (400°F) for 18 minutes and turn the wings. Take out the onions after 8 minutes, and continue cooking. Sprinkle with fresh lemon juice and sumac if using. Serve hot.

Calories 511 Total Fat 18.4g Saturated Fat 5.6g Cholesterol 204mg Sodium 801mg Total Carbohydrate 10.7g Dietary Fibre 2.2g Total Sugars 5.2g Protein 72.1g

Cooking Time Chart

	Temperature (°F)	Time (min)		Temperature (°F)	Time (min)
VEGETABLES					
Asparagus (sliced 1-inch)	400°F	5	**Onions** (pearl)	400°F	10
Beets (whole)	400°F	40	**Parsnips** (½-inch chunks)	380°F	15
Broccoli (florets)	400°F	6	**Peppers** (1-inch chunks)	400°F	15
Brussels Sprouts (halved)	380°F	15	**Potatoes** (small baby, 1.5 lbs)	400°F	15
Carrots (sliced ½-inch)	380°F	15	**Potatoes** (1-inch chunks)	400°F	12
Cauliflower (florets)	400°F	12	**Potatoes** (baked whole)	400°F	40
Corn on the cob	390°F	6	**Squash** (½-inch chunks)	400°F	12
Eggplant (1½-inch cubes)	400°F	15	**Sweet Potato** (baked)	380°F	30 to 35
Fennel (quartered)	370°F	15	**Tomatoes** (cherry)	400°F	4
Green Beans	400°F	5	**Tomatoes** (halves)	350°F	10
Kale leaves	250°F	12	**Zucchini** (½-inch sticks)	400°F	12
Mushrooms (sliced ¼-inch)	400°F	5			

	Temperature (°F)	Time (min)		Temperature (°F)	Time (min)
CHICKEN					
Breasts, bone in (1.25 lbs.)	370°F	25	**Legs, bone in** (1.75 lbs.)	380°F	30
Breasts, boneless (4 oz.)	380°F	12	**Wings** (2 lbs.)	400°F	12
Drumsticks (2.5 lbs.)	370°F	20	**Game Hen** (halved - 2 lbs.)	390°F	20
Thighs, bone in (2 lbs.)	380°F	22	**Whole Chicken** (6.5 lbs.)	360°F	75
Thighs, boneless (1.5 lbs.)	380°F	18 to 20	**Tenders**	360°F	8 to 10

BEEF

Burger (4 oz.)	370°F	16 to 20	Meatballs (3-inch)	380°F	10
Filet Mignon (8 oz.)	400°F	18	Ribeye, bone in (1-inch, 8 oz.)	400°F	10 to 15
Flank Steak (1.5 lbs.)	400°F	12	Sirloin steaks (1-inch, 12 oz.)	400°F	9 to 14
London Broil (2 lbs.)	400°F	20 to 28	Beef Eye Round Roast (4 lbs.)	390°F	45 to 55
Meatballs (1-inch)	380°F	7			

PORK AND LAMB

Loin (2 lbs.)	360°F	55	Bacon (thick cut)	400°F	6 to 10
Pork Chops, bone in (1-inch, 6.5 oz.)	400°F	12	Sausages	380°F	15
Tenderloin (1 lb.)	370°F	15	Lamb Loin Chops (1-inch thick)	400°F	8 to 12
Bacon (regular)	400°F	5 to 7	Rack of lamb (1.5 - 2 lbs.)	380°F	22

FISH AND SEAFOOD

Calamari (8 oz.)	400°F	4	Tuna steak	400°F	7 to 10
Fish Fillet (1-inch, 8 oz.)	400°F	10	Scallops	400°F	5 to 7
Salmon, fillet (6 oz.)	380°F	12	Shrimp	400°F	5
Swordfish steak	400°F	10			

FROZEN FOOD

Onion Rings (12 oz.)	400°F	8	Fish Sticks (10 oz.)	400°F	10
Thin French Fries (20 oz.)	400°F	14	Fish Fillets (½-inch, 10 oz.)	400°F	14
Thick French Fries (17 oz.)	400°F	18	Chicken Nuggets (12 oz.)	400°F	10
Mozzarella Sticks (11 oz.)	400°F	8	Breaded Shrimp	400°F	9
Pot Stickers (10 oz.)	400°F	8			

Cooking Conversions Chart

Volume: Liquid Conversion

Metric	Imperial	USA
250ml	8 fl oz	1 cup
150ml	5 fl oz	2/3 cup
120ml	4 fl oz	1/2 cup
75ml	2 1/2 fl oz	1/3 cup
60ml	2 fl oz	1/4 cup
15ml	1/2 fl oz	1 tablespoon
180ml	6 fl oz	3/4 cup

Weight Conversion

1/2 oz	15 grams
2 oz	60 grams
4 oz	110 grams
5 oz	140 grams
6 oz	170 grams
7 oz	200 grams
8 oz	225 grams
9 oz	255 grams
10 oz	280 grams
11 oz	310 grams
12 oz	340 grams
13 oz	370 grams
14 oz	400 grams
15 oz	425 grams
1 lb	450 grams

Spoons

16 tablespoons	1 cup
1 tablespoon	1/16 cup
12 tablespoons	3/4 cup
2 tablespoons	1/8 cup
10 tablespoons	2/3 cup
4 tablespoons	1/4 cup
5 tablespoons	1/3 cup
8 tablespoons	1/2 cup

Flour Conversion

USA	Metric	Imperial
1/2 cup	65 grams	2 1/4 oz
1/8 cup	15 grams	1/2 oz
1/4 cup	30 grams	1 oz
1/3 cup	40 grams	1 1/2 oz
1 cup	125 grams	4 1/2 oz
1/4 cup	30 grams	1 oz
2/3 cup	85 grams	3 oz

Porridge And Oats

USA	Metric	Imperial
1/8 cup	10 grams	1/3 oz
1 cup	85 grams	3 oz
1/4 cup	20 grams	3/4 oz
3/4 cup	60 grams	2 1/4 oz
1/3 cup	30 grams	1 oz
1/2 cup	45 grams	1 1/2 oz

Sugar

USA	Metric	Imperial
1/8 cup	25 grams	1 oz
1 cup	200 grams	7 oz
1/4 cup	50 grams	1 3/4 oz
3/4 cup	150 grams	5 1/4 oz
1/3 cup	70 grams	2 1/4 oz
1/2 cup	100 grams	3 1/2 oz
2/3 cup	135 grams	4 3/4 oz

RECIPES INDEX

FRUIT MEALS
Air Fried Pumpkin Seeds, 72
Apples with Cinnamon, 81
Baked Mangoes, 85
Caramelized Stone Fruit, 81
Figs With Honey and Mascarpone, 78
Fruit Roll-Ups, 82
Roasted Oranges, 81

GRAIN, BEANS, LEGUMES
Air Fryer BBQ Lentil Meatballs, 44
Air Fryer Black Eyed Peas & Greens, 37
Air Fryer Chickpea Fritters with Sweet-Spicy Sauce, 39
Air Fryer Falafel, 40
Black Bean Fritters, 41
Chickpea Squash Fritters, 41
Crispy Air Fryer Chickpeas, 36
Garlic and Herb Roasted Chickpeas, 37
Lentil Balls with Zesty Rice, 43
Lentil Fritters with Garlic Sauce, 43
Lupini Beans Fritters, 40

LAMB
Air Fry Loin Lamb Chops, 71
Garlic and Rosemary Lamb Chops, 66
Lamb Chops with Dijon Garlic Marinade, 66
Lamb Chops with Lemon Thyme and Farro Vinaigrette, 64
Lamb Chops with Orange Butter, 67
Lamb Sandwich, 91
Mint Lamb with Toasted Hazelnuts and Peas, 89
Orange Balsamic Lamb Chops, 68
Pistachio Crusted Lamb Rack, 65
Roast Lamb with Mint Sauce Glaze, 65
Roasted Lamb Rack with Lemon Cumin Crust, 70

MORE BEEF MEALS
Air Fried Steak Kebabs, 69
Beef and Lamb Kofta Lettuce Wraps, 64
Mini Greek-Style Meat loves and Arugula Salad, 63
Quick Kofta, 67
Steak Fajitas with Onions and Peppers, 89

MORE CHICKEN MEALS
Air Fryer Green Chili Chicken Bake, 54
Chicken Meatballs in Marinara Sauce, 76
Chicken Stuffing Casserole, 55
Greek Chicken and Orzo Pasta Salad, 60

MORE VEGETABLES
Air Fryer Black-Eyed Pea Dumpling Stew, 38
Air Fryer Garlic Aioli Artichokes, 32
Air Fryer Olives, Garlic & Tomatoes, 28
Air Fryer Pineapple Teriyaki Veggie Kabobs, 33
Air Fryer Roasted Vegetables with Halloumi Cheese, 34
Air Fryer Spinach, 31
Air Fryer Vegetable Kabobs, 33
Briam Greek Roasted Vegetables, 35
Garlic Parmesan Air Fryer Roasted Radishes, 31
Grilled Veggies & Couscous, 36
Mediterranean Vegetable Medley, 34

Mixed Veggies, 33
Moroccan Vegetable Couscous, 39
Roast Mix Vegetables & Feta, 35
Roasted Vegetables, 34

MUFFIN, CUPCAKES, COOKIES
Air Fryer Cookies, 78
Air Fryer Peanut Butter Cookies, 80
Air-Fryer Lime Macaroons, 79
Blueberry Banana Muffins, 74
Blueberry Muffins, 86
Carrot Raisin Muffins, 19
Chocolate Vanilla Cupcake, 80
Date Cookies, 80
Greek Almond Cookies, 75
Greek Easter Cookies, 75
Morning Glory Muffins, 18
Oatmeal Flax Muffins, 13

MUSHROOMS
Three Cheese Stuffed Mushrooms, 21

NUTS
Roasted Nuts, 76

OMELET
Air Fryer Vegetable Omelet, 16
Spinach, Feta, and Pepper Omelet, 16
Turkey Filled Omelets, 13

PANCAKES, TOASTS
Avocado and Egg Pizza Toast, 72
Cannoli Stuffed & French Toast, 23
Pancakes with Raspberry Topping, 79
Simple Breakfast Recipe, 78

PASTA, NOODLE
Garlicky Couscous, 38
PIES, CAKES
Blueberry Pie, 85
Chocolate Brownies, 86
Cinnamon-Cake Doughnut Holes, 17
Crispy Quinoa Cakes, 17
Mini Peach & Thyme Cobblers, 82
Orange Cornmeal Cake, 85

PIZZA
Air Fryer Breakfast Feta Pizza, 14

POTATOES
Air Fryer Spanish Spicy Potatoes, 29
Air Fryer Spicy Potato Wedges, 29
Coated Wedges in the Air Fryer, 28
Greek Mediterranean Loaded Potatoes, 89
Greek Smashed Potatoes, 24
Greek Style Lemon Potatoes, 24
Loaded Hash Browns, 19
Roasted Paprika Potatoes with Greek Yogurt, 20
Vegan Sweet Potato Fritters, 17
PRAWNS, SCALLOPS, CRABS

Air Fryer Fried Calamari, 47
Crab Cake Fritters, 92
Crab Sticks, 87
Old Bay Seasoned Crab Leg, 87

PUMPKIN, BUTTERNUT SQUASH
Herb Air Fryer Butternut Squash, 32
Orange-Cranberry Butternut Squash with Ginger, 31

QUINOA
Air Fryer Chicken Alfredo Quinoa Balls, 20
Air Fryer Chicken with Quinoa Salad, 25
Buffalo Quinoa Bites, 26
Buffalo Quinoa Fritters, 42
Tofu Coated with Quinoa Flakes, 26

RICE
Air Fried Rice with Sesame-Sriracha Sauce, 41
Air Fryer Egg Fried Rice, 42

ROLLS
Cabbage and Beef Rolls, 70
Stuffed Mozzarella Patties, 70

SAUSAGES
Foil Wrapped Sausage and Potatoes, 74

SHRIMP
Air Fryer Bacon-Wrapped Shrimp Tapas on Avocado Toast, 22
Bacon-Wrapped Shrimp with Pitta, 88
Coated Shrimp, 83
Pepper Chili Prawns, 52

TURKEY
Air Fryer Turkey Cutlets With Mushroom Sauce, 91
Turkey Panini, 63

ZUCCHINI
Air Fryer Healthy Zucchini Corn Fritters, 40
Air Fryer Zucchini Fries with Tzatziki Dip, 26
Cheesy Zucchini, 77

Printed in Great Britain
by Amazon

26976099R00057